Vietnam in Remission

Vietnam
in Remission

Edited by

JAMES F. VENINGA AND

HARRY A. WILMER

*Published for the Texas Committee for the Humanities
and the Institute for the Humanities at Salado
by Texas A&M University Press, College Station*

Library of Congress Cataloging in Publication Data
Main entry under title:

Vietnam in remission.

Bibliography: p.
Includes index.
1. Vietnamese Conflict, 1961–1975—United
States—Addresses, essays, lectures. I. Veninga, James F.
(James Frank), 1944–   . II. Wilmer, Harry A.,
1917–
DS558.V49   1985   959.704′33′73   84-40560
ISBN 0-89096-213-8

Manufactured in the United States of America
FIRST EDITION

Contents

Preface

THE papers in this volume originated in the symposium, "Understanding Vietnam," held in Salado, Texas, October 29–31, 1982. The symposium was sponsored by the Institute for the Humanities at Salado, a nonprofit educational organization founded in 1980 and dedicated to relating the disciplines of the humanities to public life.

The symposium was held in the largest public facility in Salado, the Stagecoach Inn, and attended by 159 people who gave up an Indian-summer weekend to analyze and reexperience the Vietnam War. They came with considerable misgivings, unsure of the level of confrontation that might ensue and of their ability to relieve the confusion and sorrow of that troubled time; yet they were driven by a desire to know more. In an article for the *Dallas Morning News* (November 7, 1982), reporter Allen Pusey wrote:

> There was a schoolteacher from Plano, a lawyer from Santa Fe, a psychiatrist from Albany, a United Methodist minister from Killeen and a retired general who led part of the invasion of Cambodia. They were led through the [Vietnam] experience by a history professor, a retired general, a presidential advisor, a television producer, two journalists and a poet. And among them . . . were the Vietnam veterans themselves. Each had a singular vision of the Vietnam era. With the coolness of a decade's distance, they rekindled their own images of the era. They made judgments. Not all agreed. But the fire could still be seen, burning in the distance; Vietnam has been in remission, but it has not gone away.

The presentations given at Salado by historian George C. Herring, General Douglas Kinnard, presidential advisor Walter W. Rostow, psychiatrist Harry A. Wilmer, journalist Philip L. Geyelin, and antiwar activist and poet Robert Bly, are included in this volume. Symposium evaluator Lynda E. Boose, a member of the En-

glish faculty at the University of Texas at Austin, has faithfully summarized the volatile discussion that occurred, especially between
veterans and speakers, as well as the ideas and attitudes of many of
the people attending the symposium.

It is a difficult, perhaps impossible task to draw "lessons" from
the Vietnam experience, despite philosopher George Santayana's
admonition that "those who cannot remember the past are condemned to repeat it." But Geyelin noted in an article for the *Washington Post* (November 6, 1982) that although "Salado is a far piece
from the place where policy is made. . . . it might not be a bad
place for the policymakers of the moment to repair to from time to
time to contemplate their handiwork." In a democratic tradition
much older than their country, a small group of United States citizens sought to understand the workings of government and the
consequences of a public policy—a land war in Southeast Asia
fought by American soldiers—on the lives of ordinary people.

Lawyer and writer Maury Maverick, in response to his attend-
ance at the symposium, asked the right questions in an article for
the *San Antonio Express-News* (November 7, 1982): "Why do we
make our Vietnam veterans walk alone in the shadow [of Vietnam]?
Why is it they are outcasts in their own country when they did our
bidding?"

The following papers provide some answers to these questions.
From very different perspectives, the papers offer the reader
deeper insight into the rationale for American involvement in Vietnam, the roots of our failure, and the devastating cost of military
and political policies that, however well intentioned, went awry.
The title chosen for the book, suggested by the *Dallas Morning
News* review quoted above, seems to capture the spirit of the symposium and of the book. It is true that a great deal of pain and
suffering that are still present comes through in the essays and discussions, and it is true that we are not "over" Vietnam. But is that
not what "remission" means? The disease has been checked, but
the body is not cured or whole.

Douglas Kinnard notes in his paper that the Vietnam War represents "one of the greatest failures of American foreign policy in
our time." And Philip Geyelin points out that "we owe it to those

who have sacrificed themselves in good faith, believing with good reason in the rightness of their sacrifice," to try to understand the war in Vietnam. This collection of papers is presented in that spirit.

James F. Veninga
Austin, Texas

Acknowledgments

THE idea for a public symposium on Vietnam grew out of discussion among the board members of the Institute for the Humanities at Salado. To assist with planning, an advisory committee was formed, composed of Robert Abzug, Wayne Baden, Liz Carpenter (who handled public relations), Frank Doremus, H. Tristram Engelhardt, Durwood Fleming, Thelma Fletcher, Betty Flowers, Grace Jones, Jack Knox, William Livingston, Harry Middleton, Polly Miller, Edmund Pincoffs, Patsy Sanford, Mac Sherrill, and Jane Wilmer. Professors Abzug and Flowers, both of the University of Texas at Austin, served as humanities advisors.

In addition to the plenary sessions and the formal presentations by the speakers, the symposium featured ample time for small group discussions held in the homes of Salado's citizens. These humanities teachers and writers served as discussion leaders: Betty Flowers, Robert Abzug, Wayne Baden, Frank Doremus, Harry Middleton, Edmund Pincoffs, Gaines Post, Jr., Alan Ross, Patsy Sanford, and Paul Woodruff. The hosts for these meetings were Kay and Wayne Baden, Thelma Fletcher, Alice Giles, Ruth and Pete Howe, Grace Jones, Miriam and Jack Knox, Hugh Lackey, Lola Mae and Jack McNeill, Polly and William Miller, Lucille and Cliff Pyle, Patsy and Paul Sanford, Mac Sherrill, Jaci and Kenneth Simmons, and Jane and Harry Wilmer.

The symposium was supported by grants from the Rockwell Fund, Houston; the Harris Foundation, Chicago; the Kempner Fund, Galveston; the Sarah Blaffer Foundation, Houston; the Hogg Foundation, Austin; the Texas Committee for the Humanities, a state program of the National Endowment for the Humanities; and generous donations from the members of the board of trustees of the Institute for the Humanities at Salado.

Daniel Greene, a graduate student in the Department of History at the University of Texas at Austin, provided valuable assistance in the preparation of the bibliography contained in this volume.

Dennis Darling, a faculty member in the Department of Journalism at the University of Texas at Austin, served as symposium photographer, and several of his photographs are included in the book.

The small town of Salado proved to be a marvelously suitable place of retreat where symposium speakers and audience members listened to and talked with one another, thereby contributing to the process of healing the Vietnam nightmare. The beautiful village and its hospitable people helped make the symposium a memorable experience.

Harry A. Wilmer
Salado, Texas

Perspectives on American Involvement in Vietnam

GEORGE C. HERRING

Roots of American Involvement and Failure: 1950–65

IN order to put American involvement in Vietnam into perspective, we must at the outset raise and attempt to answer two fundamental questions: Why did we become so deeply involved in Vietnam? Why did we fail to achieve our stated objectives? Coming to grips with these questions, quite obviously, is no simple undertaking. The Indochina wars spanned more than three decades. They were enormously complex, involving matters of internal Vietnamese politics, relations among the major Communist powers, and the connections of the United States with both. They pose multidimensional problems that do not lend themselves to easy answers. Moreover, we are still very close to the events; we lack the distance to see things as clearly as we would like. Much of the documentation is still unavailable on our side—and obviously on the other side as well. The basic issues are still laden with controversy.

Nevertheless, it is urgent that we deal with these questions. Vietnam has already exerted a profound influence on the way we look at ourselves and the world, and if the experience of World Wars I and II is repeated, it may exert even greater influence at some point in the future. It is vital therefore that we try to understand our experience in Vietnam and learn from it while recognizing that its "lessons" may not be directly applicable in future situations. In order to answer these questions, moreover, we must go back to the beginning. Our collective memories are notoriously short, and the further we get from events the more myopic we become. I will contend here, without taking anything away from the distinguished speakers who follow me, that we must look to the earlier years, the period 1950–65, to find the roots of our involvement—and of our ultimate failure.

Roots of Involvement

Let me turn then to the first and most basic question—why the United States committed billions of dollars and thousands of lives to an area as remote and seemingly as insignificant as Vietnam. The question of causation in war is always complex, and in the case of Vietnam, it was especially so. Our direct involvement in the Indochina wars spanned a quarter of a century. Our commitment there deepened gradually, incrementally through a series of phases. There was never a direct, immediate threat to American security or a single dramatic event that symbolized such a threat: no *Maine*, no Pearl Harbor. As many as six decisions between 1945 and 1965 account for our ultimate full-scale intervention. In each instance, alternatives were presented, but rejected. Had we taken a different route at any of these critical junctures, the outcome could have been significantly different. Amidst this complexity, then, we must attempt to single out the common threads, the modes of thought and action that determined the fateful course we chose.

Our involvement in Vietnam resulted in the broadest sense from the interaction of two post–World War II phenomena: decolonization—the breakup of the old colonial empires—and the cold war. The rise of nationalism in the colonial areas and the weakness of the colonial powers combined at the end of World War II to destroy a colonial system that had been an established feature of world politics for centuries. Obviously, a change of this magnitude did not occur smoothly or easily. It brought turmoil, conflict, and war in many areas, and we are still grappling with its consequences. The British and Dutch recognized the inevitable and adapted as best they could, granting independence to their Southeast Asian colonies shortly after World War II. The French, on the other hand, refused to concede the inevitability of decolonization. They attempted to manipulate Indochinese nationalism to their own ends, and to put down the Vietnamese revolution by force. Thus began in 1946 a war that would not end until Saigon fell in the spring of 1975.

What was unique—and ultimately from our standpoint most significant—about Vietnam was that the nationalist movement, the Vietminh, was dominated by Communists. There is no simple explanation why this was the case. The Communists enjoyed extraordinary leadership in the person of Ho Chi Minh. In marked contrast to the numerous other nationalistic groups in Vietnam, the Vietminh were well organized and tightly disciplined. They had learned from a premature uprising in the 1930s, brutally suppressed by the French, the necessity of mobilizing the peasantry to gain mass support for the revolution. They skillfully adapted Marxist ideology to traditional Vietnamese political culture. During World War II the Communists showed themselves to be particularly opportunistic. They ably exploited anti-French and anti-Japanese sentiment to build support for the cause. They moved adeptly to fill the power vacuum left when the Japanese surrendered in August, 1945. In the confusing months that followed they skillfully played the French and Chinese against each other to improve their position. They used the ensuing war with France to solidify their claim to the mantle of Vietnamese nationalism.

Of all the former European colonies in Asia—and indeed in Africa—only in Vietnam was the nationalist movement directed by Communists. Their participation would have enormous long-term implications, eventually transforming what began as a struggle against French colonialism into a major international conflict. At the very time the Communist-dominated Vietminh was engaged in a bloody anticolonial war with France, the cold war between the United States and the Soviet Union was taking form. By 1950, the Soviet-American conflict had assumed the dangerous proportions of an ideological and power struggle with global dimensions. The conjunction of these historical trends explains our involvement in Vietnam.

From at least 1949 on, we viewed the struggle in Indochina largely in terms of the cold war with the Soviet Union. We viewed Ho Chi Minh and the Vietminh as instruments of the Soviet drive for world domination, directed and controlled by the Kremlin. This viewpoint was firmly rooted in the American mind as early as 1946, and it was not seriously questioned, inside or outside of government, until we were involved in full-scale war.

Was this assessment valid? Our limited knowledge of the foreign policies of the Communist nations leaves many questions unanswered, but it seems clear that reality was more complex than we perceived it. That Ho and his top lieutenants were Communists is beyond question. That they would seize the first opportunity to establish in Vietnam a state based on Marxist-Leninist doctrine seems equally clear. It is also clear that from 1949 to 1973 China and the Soviet Union assisted the Vietminh and North Vietnam in various ways and in varying degrees of intensity. This being said, our perception of the Vietnamese revolution as a mere extension of the Communist drive for world conquest needs qualification at several points. For example, Ho initiated the revolution without explicit direction from Moscow and sustained it until 1949 without *any* external support. Moreover, the revolution drew its strength because it was able to identify with Vietnamese nationalism, the struggle to secure independence from France. Thus it had a momentum and drive of its own, quite apart from international communism. This factor was probably decisive in its ultimate success.

In addition, the support provided by the Soviet Union and China throughout the thirty-year war was neither unlimited nor unequivocal, and there is ample evidence to affirm that the three nations did not share unanimity of purpose and method. The Soviet Union exerted little influence on the revolution and provided little assistance to the Vietnamese Communists until the United States initiated the bombing of North Vietnam in 1965. Inasmuch as the Russians helped Hanoi from this point on, they apparently did so to weaken and embarrass the United States and to counter Chinese influence with Hanoi. But the Kremlin never appears to have been firmly committed to North Vietnam's overriding goal of liberating the south, and it supported Hanoi only to the extent that such support did not jeopardize more important foreign-policy goals. Even more than the Soviets, the Chinese probably preferred a weak and divided Vietnam to a strong, unified Vietnam, especially if the latter were under Soviet influence. They, too, never permitted support for Hanoi to endanger more important foreign-policy goals. Thus in 1954 at Geneva the two major Communist powers forced on Hanoi a settlement providing for the partition of Vietnam, and they gave nothing more than lip service to the provisions of the

Geneva agreement calling for the unification of the country. At another critical juncture in 1972, both the Soviets and Chinese gave lukewarm support to Hanoi, again leaving it to its own devices. As a consequence, while North Vietnam was able to play off one Communist power against the other to get the support it needed, it was keenly aware that it could not depend upon its allies. Moreover, the North Vietnamese were always fearful that dependence could lead to domination, and historic fears of Chinese domination loomed especially large in their minds. "I would rather sniff French dung for a few years than eat Chinese for a lifetime," Ho commented in 1946, rationalizing his decision to negotiate with France. This resentment of dependence carries over to the present. The fiercely nationalistic Vietnamese display open hostility toward the Russians on whom they rely for survival; they contemptuously call the Russians "Americans without money." Thus the complex, triangular relationship between the three Communist nations appears to have been based on a normal, competitive pattern of relations among nation-states rather than upon ideological harmony and shared goals. Our assessment of the dynamics of the conflict in Vietnam appears to have been off the mark.

This seems much clearer in retrospect than it did at the time, of course, and for nearly twenty years we viewed the conflict in Vietnam as an integral part of our broader worldwide struggle with communism. From this flowed yet another key assumption—that the fall of Vietnam to communism would endanger interests we deemed vital. There is more than a bit of irony here, for up to 1941 Vietnam had been of no particular significance to the United States, a position to which it has quickly reverted in the aftermath of the war. Why it had suddenly assumed such importance is therefore an especially intriguing and difficult question to answer.

In attempting to answer it, we must look first to the reorientation of American foreign policy after the fall of China to the Communists in 1949, and to the emergence of a world view best expressed in National Security Council Memorandum Number 68 (NSC–68), which posited that the Soviet Union, "animated by a new fanatical faith," was "seeking to impose its absolute authority on the rest of the world." It had already achieved major gains in Eastern Europe and more recently in China, and American policymakers concluded in the frantic milieu of early 1950 that Soviet expansion had reached a point beyond which it could not be permitted to go. "Any substantial further extension of the area under the control of the Kremlin," NSC–68 warned, "would raise the possibility that no coalition adequate to confront the Kremlin with greater strength could be assembled." In this context of a world divided into two hostile power blocs, a fragile power balance, a zero-sum game in which any gain for communism was automatically a loss for the United States, areas such as Vietnam that had been of no more than marginal importance suddenly took on great significance. Faced with this threat, and with the onset of the Korean War, which seemed to confirm the assumptions of NSC–68, the Truman administration in 1950 extended to the Far East a containment policy that to this point had been restricted to Europe. Our original commitment in Vietnam to assist the French in putting down the Vietminh revolution was part of a broader effort to contain Communist expansion in Asia.

There were other more specific reasons why American policymakers attached growing significance to Vietnam after 1950. The first, usually called the domino theory, was the idea that the fall of Vietnam could quickly lead to the fall of all of Indochina and then to the rest of Southeast Asia, with repercussions extending west to India and east to Japan and the Philippines. This fear of a political chain reaction probably originated in Hitler's sweep across Western Europe in 1940 and was reinforced by Stalin's rapid conquest of Eastern Europe after World War II. Usually associated with Eisenhower, who first publicly employed the metaphor, the theory was initially set forth as a justification for involvement in Vietnam by the Joint Chiefs of Staff in early 1950, and it was firmly rooted in the Truman years. Conditions in the Far East in the early 1950s gave it credence. Mao Zedong's Communists had just taken over in China. The departure of the colonial powers seemed to leave a gaping vacuum in Southeast Asia. Indochina, Burma, and Malaya were swept by revolution. The newly independent government of Indonesia appeared highly vulnerable. The emergence of a new and apparently ominous threat in China and the seeming vulnerability of Southeast Asia combined to produce the assumption that the fall of one area could quickly lead to the fall of others. Because of its location on China's southern border and because it appeared in the most imminent danger, Vietnam was considered the most important. Unquestionably, memories of 1941 when Japan had used Indochina as the springboard for conquest of Southeast Asia reinforced this assumption. Vietnam thus appeared "the keystone to the arch," or as Senator John Kennedy put it, "the finger in the dike." If it fell, all of Southeast Asia might be lost. The United States would lose access to important raw materials and naval bases; its strategic position throughout the Far East would be endangered. Primarily for this reason, the United States went to the aid of France in 1950 despite its great reluctance to identify itself with European colonialism, and it stepped into the breach when France was defeated in 1954.

In the Truman and Eisenhower years, the domino theory provided a basic rationale for commitment in Vietnam. In the Kennedy-Johnson years, it was reinforced and to a degree supplanted by the notion that the United States must stand firm in Vietnam to demonstrate its determination to defend vital interests. Acceptance of this principle of credibility reflects the intensity of the cold war in the 1960s, the influence of certain perceived lessons of history, the so-called Munich analogy, and the desire on the part of American policymakers to find means of averting nuclear catastrophe. The period from 1958 at least through 1963 was the period of most intense conflict during the entirety of the cold war. Confrontation was the pattern—in Laos, Berlin, Cuba, the Congo—and the possibility of nuclear war loomed large. It was entirely natural for policymakers to feel, in this context, that what they did in one area of the world might have a decisive impact in others—that if they showed firmness it might deter the adversary but if they showed weakness the enemy would be tempted to adventures which might leave no option but nuclear war.

The lessons of history—in particular, the so-called Manchurian or Munich analogy—reinforced the idea of credibility. The analogy indicated failure of the western democracies to stand firm against Japanese and German aggression had encouraged them to undertake further aggression until World War II was the result. The fundamental lesson was obvious: in order to avoid war, you must stand firm against aggression at the outset. Lyndon Johnson expressed the idea in a characteristically forthright fashion and with a particularly compelling metaphor: "If you let a bully come into your yard one day, the next day he'll be up on your porch, and the day after that he'll rape your wife in your own bed."

Even after the Sino-Soviet split dramatically altered the traditional contours of the cold war, the notion of credibility seemed to be valid. Although it is easy to forget in the aftermath of our recent "friendship" with China, in the mid-1960s, of the two Communist powers, China seemed to be the more militant and aggressive, the more deeply committed to world revolution. China was then closely allied with North Vietnam; indeed, some U.S. policymakers viewed Hanoi as essentially an instrument of Chinese policy. North Vietnam had to be deterred to prevent the expansion of Chinese influence in Asia. Even toward the Soviet Union, which seemed somewhat reticent in the aftermath of the missile crisis, there appeared to be good reason for the United States to display firmness. Rivalry with China might force the Soviets once again to assume a more aggressive posture. A firm stand in Vietnam might discourage any tendency toward a return to adventurism and reinforce the trend toward detente. It would discourage other troublemakers like Castro who were attempting to disrupt world order.

In searching for the roots of our commitment to Vietnam, we should note one other factor, the assumption shared by administrations from Truman to Johnson that the fall of Vietnam to communism would have disastrous consequences at home. Some authorities indeed claim that domestic politics was the "essential domino," the overriding source of our involvement.[1] This stemmed from other perceived lessons of history, the rancorous and divisive debate that followed the fall of China to Communism in 1949 and Republican exploitation of it at the polls in 1952. The conclusion, again obvious, was that no administration, particularly a Democratic administration, could survive the loss of Vietnam. Although a Democrat, Kennedy himself had chastised Truman for "losing" China. He had been a participant in the debate and vividly remembered it. He appears to have been sufficiently frustrated by Viet-

---

[1] Leslie Gelb, "The Essential Domino: American Politics and Vietnam," *Foreign Affairs* 50 (April, 1972): 459–75.

nam in late 1963 that he at least considered the possibility of withdrawal. But he was convinced that he could not do so until after he
had been reelected. "If I tried to pull out now," he said, "we would
have another Joe McCarthy red scare on our hands." Johnson
shared similar fears. On numerous occasions, he exclaimed that he
was not going to be the president who saw "Southeast Asia go the
way China went."

In analyzing the sources of American involvement in Vietnam,
several additional comments are in order. First, it should be emphasized that Vietnam was not deemed significant in and of itself,
for its naval bases, its raw materials, or other tangible reasons. It
was important primarily because of the presumed effects its loss
would have on other areas, and for its symbolic importance. Yet the
more we stressed its importance, the more important it became,
until it actually became a test case of our credibility to opponents,
to allies, and—perhaps most important—to ourselves. The fact
that our commitment became increasingly a matter of prestige had
important, although seemingly paradoxical consequences. On the
one hand, it made extrication all the more difficult. Interests may
be easier to compromise than prestige. On the other hand, the absence of any compelling intrinsic importance in Vietnam or any direct threat to our security made it increasingly difficult to justify
the sacrifices the American people were being called upon to make.
This paradox was responsible for at least part of the division and
frustration that accompanied the war.

Second, what appears singularly striking in retrospect is that
the assumptions undergirding our involvement went virtually unquestioned for more than a decade. On occasion, to be sure, some
voice in the wilderness would ask the really tough questions, but
they were not heard—so firmly rooted were our convictions. The
world changed enormously during the 1950s and 1960s, but our
policies and assumptions remained constant.

Were these assumptions valid, or, was our involvement based
on fundamental misperceptions and miscalculations? Obviously, we
can never answer such questions definitively. I believe, however,
that the containment policy was misguided both generally and in
its specific application to Vietnam. The simplistic, black and white
assumptions from which it derived never bore much resemblance

to reality. Soviet goals were (and remain) more the product of traditional Russian nationalism than ideology. Western interaction
with the so-called Communist bloc was never a zero-sum game.
What appeared to be a major victory for the Soviet Union in China
in 1949, for example, has turned out to be a catastrophic loss. In
most parts of the world, neither the Soviet Union nor the United
States has prevailed, and pluralism has been the norm. In applying
containment to Vietnam, we drastically misjudged the internal dynamics of the conflict. We attributed the war to an expansionist
communism bent on world domination. In fact, it began as a revolution against French colonialism. Although it can never be proven
one way or the other, I suspect that we exaggerated the consequences of non-intervention. There is reason to doubt that the
domino theory would have operated if Vietnam had fallen earlier.
Nationalism has proven the most potent and enduring force in recent history, and the nations of Southeast Asia, long suspicious of
China and Vietnam, would have resisted mightily. By making the
war a test case of our credibility, moreover, we may have made its
consequences greater than they would have been otherwise. In
short, by rigidly adhering to a narrow, one-dimensional world view
without taking into account the nature and importance of local
forces, we may have placed ourselves in an untenable position.

Roots of Failure

This leads directly to my second question: Why, despite the
expenditure of billions of dollars and the loss of thousands of lives,
did we fail to achieve our objectives? It has become fashionable in
recent years to argue that we failed because we did not use our
military power decisively; Lyndon Johnson and Robert McNamara
put restrictions on the military that prevented them from winning.
Such an argument, I think, is myopic. It ignores the fact that the
military solution we sought after in 1965 followed fifteen years of
policy failure. Indeed, it may well be that the issue was settled by
the time Johnson made his fateful 1965 decisions. Conditions
within Vietnam by that time may have reached the point where the
United States could not have attained the goal of preserving an

independent, non-Communist South Vietnam at acceptable cost. We must look to this earlier period, therefore, to get a full understanding of our ultimate failure in Vietnam.

During the period between 1950 and 1965, U.S. policy went through three quite distinct phases. Between 1950 and 1954, we supported French efforts to suppress the Vietminh revolution so strongly that by 1954 we were paying nearly 80 percent of the cost of the war. From 1954–59, we helped ease the French out of Vietnam, played a key role as midwife for the birth of South Vietnam, and violating the letter and spirit of the Geneva Accords, tried to sustain an independent government below the seventeenth parallel. From 1959 to 1965, through increased economic and military aid and eventually thousands of military "advisors," we tried to help the South Vietnamese government put down the insurgency that had begun in the south in the late 1950s and by 1965 enjoyed large-scale support from North Vietnam. Each step along the way policy failed to produce the desired results, leading to escalation of the U.S. commitment. In July, 1965, Lyndon Johnson was left the unpleasant choice of putting in American combat forces or accepting South Vietnamese defeat.

Why was this so? In terms of the French war, the so-called First Indochina war, the answer seems reasonably clear. France's goal, the retention of some level of imperial control in Indochina, ran against one of the main currents of post–World War II history. Throughout Asia and Africa, nationalist revolutions eventually prevailed, and even when imperial nations were able to win wars against insurgents, as the French later did in Algeria, they were forced to abandon what they had won at great cost—they were forced to concede independence. From the time we began supporting France in 1950, we understood this problem all too well, but we could find no way to resolve it. We pressed the French to fight on until victory was attained, while at the same time urging them to promise to leave as soon as the war ended. This made little sense from their point of view, of course, and when faced with the choice of fighting for Vietnamese independence or withdrawing, the French preferred the latter.

Ironically, the French may have come closer to attaining a

short-term victory than they realized. There is evidence to suggest
that during the Dienbienphu crisis of 1954, while France was pressing the United States to intervene, Ho Chi Minh was pressing the
Chinese and even the Russians to intervene, warning that the Vietminh had suffered such heavy losses that they could not continue
the war much longer. This raises the tantalizing possibility that if
Eisenhower and Dulles had listened to the French and intervened
in 1954, a favorable settlement might have been attained without
the bloodshed and agony that followed. Possible, but I think doubt-
ful. Had we gone in, it is difficult to see how the Russians and
particularly the Chinese could have stayed out. Even if they had
stayed out, could we, with or without the French, have constructed
and sustained a viable government in fragmented, war-torn Vietnam? All of this is idle speculation, of course. The great powers did
not intervene. The Russians and Chinese imposed on the Vietminh
a settlement less favorable than they thought they were entitled to.
The United States refused to bail out the French, not primarily
because of British opposition to intervention, as has often been argued, but because we could not agree with France on goals or
methods. Even while the Geneva Conference was still on, the
United States was planning ways to exploit partition to create a
bulwark against further Communist expansion in Vietnam.

The reasons for the failure of American efforts to sustain an
independent, non-Communist South Vietnam between 1955 and
1965 are more complex and elusive, but several factors seem important. First—and perhaps foremost—was the magnitude and in-
tractability of the problem. Had we looked all over the world, we
might not have been able to choose a less-promising place for an
experiment in nation building. The economy of southern Vietnam
was shattered from ten years of war. The departure of the French
left a gaping political vacuum. The French had destroyed the traditional fabric of Vietnamese politics in the south and by establish-
ing direct imperial control left nothing to replace it. As a result,
France left behind no firmly established political tradition; no institutions of government; no native elite capable of exercising effective leadership. In addition, southern Vietnam was fragmented by
a multitude of conflicting political, religious, and ethnic groups; it
was, in the words of one scholar, a "political jungle of war lords,

bandits, partisan troops, and secret societies."[2] The immigration of nearly a million Catholics from the north after 1954 added to the already confused and conflict-ridden picture (and removed from North Vietnam a major source of dissidence). Under these circumstances, there may have been built-in limits to what the United States or any nation might have accomplished in South Vietnam.

Second, our nation-building policies were sometimes misdirected or misapplied. In the early years we focused on building an army to meet the threat of an invasion from the north, a perfectly logical step in terms of the situation in Vietnam and what had happened in Korea, but one that left the South Vietnamese ill-prepared to cope with the insurgency that erupted in the late 1950s. By contrast, too little attention was given in the first years to mobilizing the peasantry and promoting pacification in the countryside. When we attempted to meet these problems in the early 1960s, we applied techniques that had worked elsewhere but did not adapt well in Vietnam. The strategic-hamlet program of the Kennedy years is a case in point. The idea of bringing peasants from isolated villages into settlements where they could be protected had worked in Malaya. But in Malaya the insurgents were Chinese and it was relatively easy to guard against infiltration, whereas in Vietnam, the insurgents were Vietnamese who had lived and worked with the villagers for years, and the hamlets were infiltrated with relative ease. In Malaya, moreover, the peasants were resettled without major disruptions, but in Vietnam they had to be removed from lands on which their families had lived for centuries and which were regarded as sacred. Sometimes they had to be forcibly removed, their old homes burned behind them. They were left rootless and resentful, easy prey for National Liberation Front (NLF) recruiters.

A third problem—perhaps the most critical one—was that of native leadership, a problem all too clearly revealed in our frustrating and ultimately tragic partnership with Ngo Dinh Diem. In terms of his anticommunism and his nationalism, Diem appeared to fit our needs perfectly, and in the early years he seemed a mira-

---

[2]Frances Fitzgerald, *Fire in the Lake: The Vietnamese and the Americans in Vietnam* (Boston: Little, Brown, 1972), p. 69.

cle worker, stabilizing South Vietnam in a way no one thought possible. In time, however, his deficiencies became all too apparent. It was not simply or even primarily that his government was corrupt and undemocratic. Corrupt governments have survived for years and Diem may have had logic on his side when he warned that democracy would not work in Vietnam. There were other problems more basic. He was a poor administrator. He tolerated far too much from his notorious family. Most important, he lacked any real blueprint for Vietnam. He proved incapable of leading his country, mobilizing the peasantry behind his government, and coping with the insurgency.

He was also fiercely independent, and this posed a dilemma the United States never resolved. Americans in time saw his deficiencies, but they could not persuade him to change his ways and they could not impose their will on him. They saw no alternative to him, however, and feared that if they removed him it would only lead to greater chaos. Thus the United States, with some reluctance, stood by him for nine years, while the political and military situation steadily deteriorated. "Diem is Diem, but he's the best we've got," Kennedy commented. "Sink or swim with Ngo Dinh Diem," a journalist summed up American policy. It was only when Diem's policies produced a full-scale political upheaval in South Vietnam—the Buddhist crisis of 1963—when it was learned that he and his notorious brother were secretly negotiating with Hanoi, that the United States finally concluded that he must go.

As many had predicted, however, the coup of November, 1963, offered no solutions—only more problems. The generals who replaced Diem were for the most part educated in France and the United States. Out of touch with their own people, they were even less well equipped than Diem had been to unify a fragmented society. Divided among themselves, they spent their energy on intrigue and one coup followed another in such rapid fashion that it was impossible to keep up with the changes in government. Thus by mid-1965, the United States found itself in a position it had never really wanted and whose dangers it recognized—that of an imperial power moving in to fill a political and military vacuum. It was a thankless—perhaps impossible—role.

To stop here, focusing on our failure, would provide a one-sided picture. It is also necessary to note why the other side by 1956 had reached the verge of victory. We now know from captured documents that by 1957 Diem had very nearly exterminated the Vietminh who had stayed south after the Geneva agreement of 1954. Alarmed by their plight and by the certainty that the elections called for by the Geneva agreement would not be held, the remaining stay-behinds began to mobilize to salvage the Vietminh revolution of 1945. The insurgents effectively exploited the unrest caused by Diem's heavy-handed methods. In many areas they implemented land-reform programs that contrasted favorably with the policies of the government. They also employed selective violence effectively and mobilized the peasantry in many areas in a way the government had not been able to. By the early 1960s the NLF controlled large segments of the land and the population and had developed a formidable army.

North Vietnam's part in this remains a matter of controversy. It seems clear that Hanoi did not instigate the revolution in the south, as the United States government claimed at the time. Nor did it remain an innocent and even indifferent bystander, as the doves maintained. The revolution began spontaneously in the south, initially, at least, against the wishes, perhaps even against the instructions, of the Hanoi government. Once it began, however, North Vietnam could not stand by and watch. Fearful that the southern revolutionaries might fail—or succeed—without help, it began to send cadres south to assume leadership of the insurgency, giving it at least a measure of control. In 1959 Hanoi approved the initiation of "armed struggle" against the Diem government. In the aftermath of the overthrow of Diem, North Vietnam decided to undertake a major escalation of the conflict, even to the point of sending its own military units south to fight. It took this step apparently in the expectation that the United States, when faced with certain defeat, would withdraw, as it had in China in 1949, rather than risk its own men and resources.

In this, of course, the North Vietnamese gravely miscalculated. Confronting the collapse of South Vietnam in 1965, Lyndon Johnson never seriously considered the option of withdrawal. Determined to uphold a commitment of more than a decade standing and certain that tiny North Vietnam could not defy the will of the world's greatest power, Johnson first initiated the bombing of North Vietnam and then in July, 1965, committed U.S. ground forces to the struggle. In making this latter commitment, he also seriously miscalculated. He rejected the proposals of Secretary McNamara and the Joint Chiefs to mobilize the reserves. To avoid any risk of confrontation with China and Russia, and, more important, to prevent what he called "that bitch of a war" from interfering with what he termed "the woman I really loved"—the Great Society—he escalated the war as quietly as possible while imposing the lightest possible burden on the American people. He did so in the expectation that the gradual increase of military pressure on North Vietnam would bring it to its senses and persuade it to abandon the struggle in the south.

Why then did we go to war in Vietnam? We went as the result of a series of incremental commitments made over a period of fifteen years, each of which stemmed from the larger dictates of the containment policy. This policy viewed most local conflicts as deriving from the cold war. It defined all areas of the world as of equal importance. At each stage of the game, American policymakers recognized the pitfalls of escalation. Given the requirements of the containment policy, however, they saw no option but to act as they did, and at each critical juncture, they were confident, if not absolutely certain, that a large injection of American power would reverse the tide. The essential flaw of American policy was not, as many now argue, that we misused our military power, but rather than we intervened in a situation where the local forces ran against us: We supported a weak, fragmented client state against a determined, indeed fanatical, adversary in a situation where all-out war was not only risky but also likely to be counterproductive. It was a no-win situation, and the surprising thing, when viewed from a more distant perspective, may be that we persisted as long as we did in the face of such great frustration.

DOUGLAS KINNARD

The "Strategy" of the War in South Vietnam

IN my view there is little doubt that one of the greatest failures of American foreign policy in our time was what we now call the Vietnam War. Quite apart from the devastation suffered by that country, the disruption of the American political scene, the loss of lives, and the waste of resources, the American military incursion into this Asian war was such a catastrophe that we are still having problems explaining to ourselves, dispassionately, just what happened. But we need to do this so that the lessons of the tragedy will not go unheeded.

I would like to examine several military aspects that might contribute to the understanding of this problem, from the American entry into war in 1965 through the final withdrawal some eight years later. I am concerned with four specific points. In discussing strategy, I will first construct a strategic framework as a model to refer to and for stating some conclusions. Second, I want to examine the early conduct of the ground war in the south in terms of the objectives we established for ourselves. Third, I will trace, in the context of these objectives, the conduct of the war during our most active participation. Finally, I will comment on the withdrawal phase, 1969 through 1972, the so-called Vietnamization phase.

A Strategic Framework

The first point concerns strategic concepts. Strategy has many definitions, but I believe that the most relevant here is that used

This essay is based on the address given at the symposium by the author, then professor of Political Science at the University of Vermont. It was written in its present form by Dr. Alexander S. Cochran, Jr., but the concepts are General Kinnard's.

by the Joint Chiefs of Staff when the United States became a combatant in Vietnam in 1965. For them, "strategy is the art and science of developing and using the political, economic, psychological power of a nation, together with its military force to secure national objectives."[1] Thus military force is a major element, though not the exclusive part, of total strategy.

In my model there are four dimensions to this strategy. Three come from Michael Howard's conceptualization and the last is my own. The first dimension is operational, the movement of one armed force to overcome another armed force. Classic examples of this kind are the best campaigns of Napoleon—decisive victories through skillful maneuvering of forces and precise application of firepower. In his time this was what war was all about, and no one understood the operational dimension better than he.

The second dimension to strategy is logistical—a dimension to which we give all too little thought. A classic example is Gen. U.S. Grant's strategy in the American Civil War by which he wore down and eventually overpowered one of the greatest Western armies of all time, Lee's Army of Northern Virginia. Grant overwhelmed this army because he understood thoroughly the complex logistical dimension in modern strategy. I will not return to this dimension of strategy in my conclusion. It was handled by us well, perhaps too well, during the course of the Vietnam War.

The third dimension is the sociopsychological one, which became significant with the development of total war in the late nineteenth century and became more and more important during World War I and afterward. In that 1914–18 conflict, mobilization of the home fronts emerged as the key to victory. The society with the weakest home front will collapse first. One sees this especially when reading the last chapter of that greatest of all World War I novels, *All Quiet on the Western Front*, with its poignant description of the collapse of the German home front.

Finally, within my strategy model, I propose a managerial dimension of strategy. More important here even than organization and leadership is the complex field of civil-military relations. In my

---

[1] U.S. Joint Chiefs of Staff, JCS Publication 6, *Dictionary of United States Terms for Joint Usage* (Washington: Government Printing Office, 1968).

view, this, along with the sociopsychological dimension, is the critical dimension in our understanding of America's strategy in the Second Indochina War.[2]

Before examining the conduct of the war, we should recall the advice of Karl von Clausewitz in his classic tome, *On War*. "War can never be separated from political intercourse," the German philosopher of strategy wrote in the nineteenth century, "and if this occurs, we have before us a senseless thing, without an object."[3]

Early Military Objectives

Now we can turn to the American role in the conduct of the ground war in Vietnam, beginning with an emphasis on the strategic objectives that we set for ourselves at the outset of the war. While some of my findings here are based upon published sources and analyses such as Dave Palmer's *Summons of the Trumpet* and *The Pentagon Papers*, much also derives from my own experiences in that war and subsequent research and teaching.[4]

The initial test for the embryonic American strategy came in November, 1965. As part of the first sustained campaign against the North Vietnamese Army, units of the First Air Cavalry Division, in a meeting engagement, waged a particularly bloody battle at the Ia Drang River, when the enemy chose to stand and fight against the Americans. At this battle the Americans found, for the first time, their mobility and firepower matched against the manpower and choice of terrain of the North Vietnamese.

Military victory at the Ia Drang was significant for American strategists. It not only derailed Hanoi's hopes for an early victory but also gave Americans some feelings of assurance in that first dimension of strategy—operational. As a result, our goal soon became to defeat the enemy rather than merely to prevent South

[2]Douglas Kinnard, *The Secretary of Defense* (Lexington: University of Kentucky Press, 1980), chapters 3 and 4, *passim.*

[3]Karl von Clausewitz, *On War*, ed. and trans. Michael Howard and Peter Paret (Princeton: Princeton University Press, 1976).

[4]Dave Richard Palmer, *Summons of the Trumpet* (San Rafael: Presidio Press, 1978); *The Pentagon Papers: The Defense Department History of United States Decision-Making on Vietnam. The Senator Gravel Edition*, 5 vols. (Boston: Beacon Press, 1971–72).

Vietnamese defeat. Obviously, winning is different from not losing, which, until the Ia Drang victory, was the principal concern of American strategists. Now the objective was to devise a winning strategy.

What did develop in Washington, however, was not a grand strategic plan, even though *The Pentagon Papers* may give that impression. Rather, a series of programs were begun—essentially designed by American planners in Vietnam and worked over in Washington that outlined certain minigoals and the required troop increases to meet these goals. The key figure in Washington was Secretary of Defense Robert S. McNamara, who approved the force levels (as they were incrementally developed over six different programs) and the goals assigned to them.

In February, 1966, several months after the Ia Drang battles, President Lyndon B. Johnson, Secretary McNamara, and Gen. William C. Westmoreland, along with their senior aides, met in Honolulu to discuss the conduct of the war. From this conference came the well-known Honolulu Declaration, emphasizing the economic and sociological programs known as pacification. General Westmoreland also received a two-page directive that (he stated later) provided the guidance for his strategy in 1966 and beyond.[5] Not drafted by the Joint Chiefs of Staff, the memo was rather the work of two men, Deputy Secretary of Defense John McNaughton and Assistant Secretary of State William Bundy. Knowing the relationship that they had with their bosses, we may assume approval by McNamara and Dean Rusk.

This directive to the overall commander in Vietnam at a critical take-off point in the war was the one that Westmoreland used to develop his strategy. And what was that guidance? He was to increase offensive operations against the enemy, and his available combat forces were to be doubled from thirty-five to seventy-nine battalions. His objectives included increased destruction of enemy base areas, from 10 percent to 40 or 50 percent. He was also to ensure the defense of all military bases and population centers then under government control. This was not only a big task but, also,

[5]William C. Westmoreland, *A Soldier Reports* (Garden City: Doubleday, 1976), pp. 160–61.

in more than one way, a fuzzy one. How, for instance, do you destroy a base area when it might be occupied again? What does 40 to 50 percent mean in such a context?

In 1974, when I surveyed the general officers who had commanded in Vietnam, I asked: "How clear were the objectives of the war?" Here are some of their replies: "We intervened with no clear idea of where we are heading. . . . Played it by ear. . . . The objective was never clear to anyone. . . . The U.S. was committed to a military solution without a firm military objective. . . . The policy was attrition, killing Vietcong. This offered no solution—it was senseless."[6] In responding to the question, almost 70 percent of the generals said that they were uncertain of the war's objectives. While it seems possible for 70 percent of the privates in a war to be unsure of the objectives, how is it possible for 70 percent of the generals not to understand the objectives? To me, this mirrors a deep-seated strategic failure: the inability of policymakers to frame tangible, obtainable goals.

Military Conduct of the War

Now we should consider the third general point—the conduct of the war during our most active period. In 1966 what was General Westmoreland's strategy for the war, and how did its conduct influence American participation during the high tide of our stay? A critical point to be remembered here is the constraints policy. There were many constraints in Vietnam—for example, places where firepower could not be employed without clearances—but the most important check in strategy was the territorial constraint. Military forces could not operate in North Vietnam; neither, at least until very late in the war, could they operate in Laos or Cambodia. Though the constraint concerning North Vietnam is perhaps more understandable than the other two, still in aggregate, these were definite checks to General Westmoreland's operations. The constraints had the effect of reducing the scope of mission to a rather technical one. Compare that mission with the one assigned to Gen-

[6]Douglas Kinnard, *The War Managers* (Hanover: University Press of New England, 1977), pp. 24–25.

eral Eisenhower in World War II: "You will enter the continent of Europe and, in combination with allied forces, drive to the heart of Germany and destroy the German armed forces."[7]

The strategy that Westmoreland developed involved three tiers of available forces and was based on the success of firepower as demonstrated at the Ia Drang. His problem was, of course, that he could not occupy all the areas controlled by the enemy. Instead, he could only seek out the enemy in selected locations and attempt to destroy him (the operational dimension that had proven so successful in the Ia Drang). This was the origin of the strategy of the search-and-destroy mission that seemed appropriate for a war being fought in a jungle environment. This was the portion of the strategy that American units were committed to, with good success, at that stage of the war. They did, however, face a consistent problem: because of the territorial constraints, the enemy retained the precious initiative in the broadest sense—they were free to retreat across the border at any time. Still, given the focus on the operational dimension of strategy and the available forces, there seemed to be no other viable American option. As large-scale search-and-destroy operations like Cedar Falls in the old enemy base areas of the "iron triangle" north of Saigon demonstrated, they worked, but only temporarily, for the enemy returned if he wished to.

While the Americans conducted search-and-destroy missions, the regular Vietnamese forces (Army of the Republic of Viet Nam—ARVN) were assigned to provide protection in the government-controlled areas, and the local militia units were concentrated on local defense and pacification. With some oversimplification then, this was Westmoreland's three-tier strategy.

How was one to measure the success of this strategy? In linear wars, measurement was easy, especially with geographical objectives that could be seen. In World War II, an objective after securing the beachhead at Normandy was the Seine River. Thus, if at D Day plus 90, you were there, you were on time. If you weren't, you had problems. But how do you measure progress when the objective is destruction of 40 to 50 percent of enemy base areas? How does the ground commander know if his strategy is working?

---

[7]Dwight D. Eisenhower, *Crusade in Europe* (Garden City: Doubleday, 1949), p. 225.

In Vietnam the answer was a series of indicators called the Measurement of Progress system, an awkward name suggesting an upward linear curve. Indicators included control of certain roads or areas. But since the real goal was destroying the enemy, the most significant indicator was based upon the number of enemy killed: the enemy-to-friendly kill ratio, based upon body count. We were in effect engaged in a war of attrition.

By this standard we seemed to be making progress in the war from 1966 through 1967. Though American officials in both Vietnam and Washington became suspicious of the validity of the indicators, especially body count, in 1967 most of them thought our strategy was working. By July of that year, it seemed that we had reached the crossover point at which more enemy soldiers were being killed than could be replaced.

In the fall of that year, notwithstanding the constraints policy—given the increased efficiency of the South Vietnamese at the second- and third-tier levels plus the firepower supplied by the Americans at the first-tier level—our Vietnam strategy appeared to be working; it seemed to be accomplishing the objectives assigned at the Honolulu Conference. At the end of 1967 General Westmoreland announced: "In many areas, the enemy has been driven away from the population centers. In others, he has been compelled to disperse and avoid contact. The year ended with the enemy resorting to desperation tactics to achieve military psychological victory. He has experienced only failure in these attempts."[8] December, 1967, was the point in the war when American prospects for concluding it favorably seemed brightest.

However, the North Vietnamese were in the process of reassessing their own strategic situation. Gen. Vo Nguyen Giap, victor over the French at Dienbienphu in the prior decade, had a similar plan for the Americans. His notion was based upon several assumptions. He first correctly assumed that American combat-force level would not be noticeably increased. He also correctly deduced that the territorial constraints would remain in effect. And he did not forget the sociopsychological dimension of strategy. He postulated that antiwar sentiment in the United States would be a powerful political force in the upcoming election year; in fact, he believed

[8]*The Pentagon Papers*, IV, 538–39.

that it might be the decisive factor in the outcome of the war. (Time would prove that his assumption was fairly sound.) Two more assumptions—these concerning the South Vietnamese—proved incorrect. Giap thought that the South Vietnamese army would not fight when faced with a major offensive. He was wrong. Furthermore, he expected the Vietnamese people to respond with a general uprising if the Vietcong and North Vietnamese showed indications of success. Again he was wrong.

The complex plan that he came up with was, in essence, a two-tiered scheme. The first—which began in the fall of 1967 and peaked in early January, 1968—involved a series of diversionary attacks along the border areas, in particular Khe Sanh. Giap's intent was to focus American attention, interest, and resources away from his major objective of a general offensive. Though his tactic proved extremely expensive in terms of manpower, he had dismissed that consideration earlier when he wrote: "The life and death of a hundred, or a thousand, or tens of thousands of human beings, even if they were our own compatriots, represents very little."[9] Thus, in terms of his goals, his losses became irrelevant. Though he had to face public opinion in his own country, this factor was not as constraining as that faced by his counterparts in the United States. The second part of his plan was a series of simultaneous attacks throughout the country. Problems of coordination made them difficult to stage, but they did achieve their overall objective in spectacular fashion. His plan was to launch simultaneous attacks on Tet, the first day of the lunar New Year in Vietnam. On January 30, 1968, General Giap's offensive began. Within a day, North Vietnamese and Vietcong forces had attacked 36 of the 44 provincial capitals in South Vietnam, 5 of the 6 autonomous cities, and the capital, Saigon. At the same time, 64 of the 240 district capitals were assaulted, along with 50 hamlets.

What General Giap had in mind with this two-tier strategy was a psychological blow—a denial of the great progress being reported to the American people. In 1967 this message had been personally carried back by General Westmoreland to his commander in chief, Lyndon Johnson, who desperately required public assurance that the war was going well. Using vital statistics, the senior commander

[9]Palmer, *Summons*, p. 168.

in Vietnam made glowing progress reports to American audiences that included a joint session of the Congress in April and the National Press Club in November. It was with confidence that the American people turned on their television sets on January 30 and February 1: they were shocked to find enemy troops openly fighting in South Vietnamese cities and towns throughout the country and indeed on the grounds of the American Embassy itself.

General Giap's Tet Offensive of 1968 was an audacious plan, stunning in execution and vast in its repercussions. It was the highpoint in military action of the Second Indochina War. When all other battles of that war are forgotten, Tet 1968 will be remembered. Afterward, nothing was the same.

In military terms, Tet proved to be a technical defeat for the North Vietnamese and Vietcong. They failed to hold any province capital, in some instances only lingering long enough to run up a flag and then take it down after American television cameras had recorded the standard. They paid a terrible price in terms of casualties. Not by accident, the Vietcong bore the brunt, with over forty thousand guerrillas killed. Generations of jungle fighters were wiped out, now to be replaced by cadres from the north. Yet, psychologically, it was a tremendous victory over the United States, for Americans looked at their television sets in disbelief. "How," they now asked, "after all these years of favorable kill ratios and glowing progress reports, could a bunch of kids in sneakers be running through the American Embassy?" Of course, they were just running to their own deaths, but their visual presence proved devastating on the American home front. The domestic pressure that arose in the wake of Tet brought on the abdication speech of a president, a curtailment of bombing in the North, and the opening of cease-fire negotiations in Paris. What Dienbienphu had done to the French home front in 1953, Tet did to the American in 1968. It fostered a new direction in American strategy.

Vietnamization

The origins for this new strategy—Vietnamization—came during the presidential campaign of 1968. One of Richard Nixon's campaign promises was that he "had a plan to get us out of Vietnam." As this amorphous pledge underlay his victory, one of his first steps as president was to query the members of the National Security community on Vietnam strategy. This document, National Security Study Memorandum Number 1, which contained some twenty-eight questions about Vietnam, was written and coordinated by Henry Kissinger. Based on the responses and Kissinger's analysis, the Nixon administration restructured the Vietnam strategy into two new goals. [10]

The first goal, one Lyndon Johnson hoped to achieve, was to negotiate a Vietnam cease-fire. In this context we should remember that there were two kinds of negotiations, "formal" and "real." The formal negotiations were discussions held on a regular basis in Paris; they focused upon nominal matters that at the outset included the shape of the negotiation table. The real negotiations were discussions between Kissinger and Le Duc Tho on substantive issues, conducted on a more episodic basis at private locations.

Nixon's second strategic goal, Vietnamization, was the concern of defense officials in Washington and Saigon. Basically, the objective was to replace Americans with Vietnamese, not only in the military forces but also in the supply and support troops. Responsibility for implementing the policy fell to the new secretary of defense, Melvin Laird, and the new commander in Vietnam, Gen. Creighton Abrams. Tremendous effort went into Vietnamization in both Washington and Saigon and, at first, things seemed to be going pretty well. By late 1969 and early 1970, American forces were, in fact, turning over the main war to the Vietnamese forces. Of course, another factor at work here was that the North Vietnamese and Vietcong themselves were still recovering from their own previous losses.

Still there were skeptics about Vietnamization among the South Vietnamese officials. The day before I left Vietnam in 1970, I had lunch with a South Vietnamese general, then commanding a division; he saw no chance for Vietnamization success. To him, it was a clear case of an American cut-and-run operation. Bureaucratic efforts and political realities in Washington proved more crucial than oriental doubts in Saigon, especially since the president was committed to having all American combat troops out of Viet-

---

[10]Henry Kissinger, *White House Years* (Boston: Little, Brown, 1979), p. 238.

nam by 1972. When the first goal of his strategy—cease-fire negotiations—stalled, the second objective—Vietnamization—seemed
to be well on track. Certainly a great deal of credit for this goes to
Secretary of Defense Melvin Laird, who convinced the military
that removal of American forces from Vietnam was the best course
for the future. In the efforts at Vietnamization, frequently occurring
faster than Kissinger wanted, General Abrams proved the key military figure, loyally and effectively supporting the defense secretary.

In retrospect, however, three specific military actions taught
hard lessons about the weakness of the Vietnamization strategy.
The first came out of the Cambodian incursion of May, 1970, when,
for the first time in the Vietnam ground war, territorial constraints
against American ground troops were lifted. The premise was that
if enough enemy supplies were destroyed, precious time would be
gained for the Vietnamization strategy to take root. We were tech-
nically successful. Still, few in charge in Washington reflected on
how dependent the Vietnamese forces had been upon vital American firepower—both air and artillery—for that success.

The second military action that provides a lesson on Vietnamization was Lam Son 719, the South Vietnamese operation in February, 1971. The objective here was to sever the vital North Vietnamese supply route, the Ho Chi Minh Trail, by striking from the
northern provinces of South Vietnam into Laos. During the initial
phases, when American firepower was provided, all went well for
the Vietnamese. But when Vietnamese forces entered Laos and territorial constraints forced the Americans to withdraw their firepower, the operations ground to a halt. Eventually the South Vietnamese forces pulled back; it was to be their last major offensive
operation of the war.

The final military action that provides a lesson on Vietnamization was the North Vietnamese campaign in mid-1972, the so-called
Easter Offensive. Here General Giap entered into conventional
strategy for the first time in the war, attacking from both north and
west. Open warfare ensued, with the South Vietnamese prevailing,
though now from a defensive posture. The critical factor again was
American firepower, this time B–52 air strikes. However, the North
Vietnamese were permitted to retain their incursions into the ter-

ritory of South Vietnam. This was not only the final blow to our Vietnamization strategy but also our last military action in that protracted conflict. Fast on the heels of the Easter Offensive came the Paris cease-fire accords and the removal of the last U.S. forces from Vietnam.

It is now clear that these three military actions demonstrated to those who cared to listen that, without American firepower, the South Vietnamese forces simply could not handle the North Vietnamese, either offensively or defensively. Even at the time, I do not think that anyone who knew what was going on ever really thought that the South Vietnamese could.

The final collapse was to come several years later, after an "indecent interval." Thus ended one of America's greatest foreign- and military-policy failures.

Some Lessons

In conclusion, I return to my earlier point about the dimensions of strategy, relating them to the conduct of the war. I would like to extrapolate some impressionistic lessons from our Vietnam strategy.

Regarding the operational dimension, I believe that there are two lessons. One, there was a definite lack of clarity concerning our objectives; this severely crippled the strategy involving military operations. Two, we were fighting a war of attrition in which the enemy retained the initiative as to when and where he would fight. It thus became a war of wills, not a war of power. Unfortunately, while we had the power, the enemy retained the initiative and had the will.

There are two lessons to be drawn from the sociopsychological dimension of strategy. First, American planners forgot a lesson that they had earlier learned in the Korean War—America simply cannot handle a long and inconclusive war whose objectives are not clear. Those planning the war in Saigon did not consider American public opinion their responsibility. While consideration of public opinion should have been largely the responsibility of those in Washington, American planners in Saigon also needed to pay attention to it. Second, those planners also failed to appreciate the role of the media in Vietnam, especially that of television. To sustain part-time visual interest of an event over a long period of time requires sensationalism. To put this in a broader context, suppose that television had covered the landings at Omaha Beach on D Day, June 7, 1944, when the Twenty-sixth Infantry Regiment, First Infantry Division—a force of 3,000 officers and men—required replacement of 70 officers and 800 enlisted men after twenty-four hours of combat. What effect would this have had on World War II, especially if repeated day in and day out on American television? Planners and strategists in the future must consider and deal with the media, especially television, which they cannot censor. They must acknowledge this sociopsychological force when they decide on the kind and probable length of a war.

For the managerial dimension of strategy, in my view, there is one overriding lesson. In developing this, we must consider the pivotal position of the secretary of defense, who provided the interface between military and civilian officials. It was in this office that the key decisions were made on Vietnam. Secretary McNamara operated under some difficult domestic constraints based on presidential perceptions. His Great Society programs dominated Johnson's views, which meant budget manipulations, no public debate, and no reserve call-ups. He also faced external constraints on the conduct of the war, chiefly the very genuine concern over Chinese and Soviet reactions. Bearing in mind these internal and external checks, some military writers have placed the blame for the outcome of the war on "inexperienced civilians." To a degree they are correct. Inexperience among civilians there was, but, in my judgment, this led to the military commanders having *too much*, not *too little*, leeway in running the war. From June, 1965, on, General Westmoreland was pretty much in position to fight any kind of war he wished in Vietnam within the constraints policy. Even when Secretary McNamara became disenchanted with the military approach in Vietnam, he chose to keep his peace and did not speak out against his senior field commander. Given the lack of meaningful guidance from Washington on the conduct of the ground war (in contrast to detailed guidance on the air war), Westmoreland was probably correct in interpreting such as approval of the way he was conducting the ground war. The critical failure here was that of the civilians to become more involved with the pivotal question—what we were really doing in Vietnam—rather than with what the next troop increase was to be.

I end with a quotation from W. H. Auden's "Spain" that conveys to me the sense of waste and loss that was the Second Indochina War:

> History to the defeated
> May say Alas but cannot help nor pardon.

WALTER W. ROSTOW

The Strategic Significance of
Vietnam and Southeast Asia

The Neglected Issue

The United States involvement in Vietnam and Southeast Asia had and has many dimensions in that region and at home: military and economic, social and political, human and moral. I tried to evoke the multiple facets of the problem in the relevant passages of my book, *The Diffusion of Power.*[1]

I decided, however, that on this occasion I could be most useful if I focused on one important and largely neglected aspect of the subject: the strategic significance to all the relevant powers of Southeast Asia.

In their serious effort to analyze the U.S. involvement in Vietnam, Leslie Gelb and Richard Betts take as their central thesis the following proposition: ". . . U.S. leaders considered it vital not to lose Vietnam by force to communism. They believed Vietnam to be vital, not for itself, but for what they thought its 'loss' would mean internationally and domestically."[2]

George Herring's interesting assessment contains a brief, accurate passage evoking the reasons for anxiety about Southeast Asia in Washington in the wake of the Communist takeover of China in 1949;[3] but so far as my reading of his book revealed, there is no further discussion of the strategic importance of Vietnam or Southeast Asia.

[1] New York: Macmillan, 1972.
[2] Leslie H. Gelb with Richard K. Betts, *The Irony of Vietnam: The System Worked* (Washington, D.C.: The Brookings Institution, 1979), p. 25.
[3] George C. Herring, *America's Longest War: The United States and Vietnam, 1950–1975* (New York: John Wiley, 1979), pp. 10–12.

The general view of those who opposed U.S. policy towards Southeast Asia in the 1960s is quite well captured by John Kenneth Galbraith's bon mot of April 25, 1966: "If we were not in Vietnam, all that part of the world would be enjoying the obscurity it so richly deserves."[4] Or, take the following passages from a 1968 interview with Eugene McCarthy in the *New York Times*:

> I [interviewer] asked him [McCarthy] the final question about Vietnam: "How are we going to get out?" He said, "Take this down. I said that the time has come for us to say to the Vietnamese, we will take our steel out of the land of thatched huts, we will take our tanks out of the land of the water buffalo, our napalm and flame-throwers out of the land that scarcely knows the use of matches. We will give you back your small and willing women, your rice-paddies and your land." He smiled. "That's my platform. It's pretty good, isn't it?"[5]

At first glance, there would appear to be some evidence for the view that the U.S. government did not regard Vietnam as being of intrinsic importance; for example, neither in office nor in their memoirs did Richard Nixon or Henry Kissinger discuss Southeast Asian policy except as an inherited burden and a responsibility that had to be honored if the credibility of U.S. guarantees elsewhere was to be sustained. As I shall note later, John Kennedy and Lyndon Johnson (but not all members of their administrations) took a different view. The fact is that over the past forty years nine successive presidents—from Franklin Roosevelt to Ronald Reagan—have made serious strategic commitments to the independence of Southeast Asia, in every case with some pain and contrary to other interests.

The story begins, in a sense, with this passage from Cordell Hull's memoirs, which is where the Pentagon Papers should have begun but didn't:

> . . . Japanese troops on July 21 [1941] occupied the southern portions of Indo-China and were now in possession of the whole of France's strategic province, pointing like a pudgy thumb toward the Philippines, Malaya, and the Dutch East Indies. . . .
> When Welles telephoned me, I said to him that the invasion of

---

[4]Compiled by William G. Efros, *Quotations Vietnam: 1945–1970* (New York: Random House, 1970), p. 51.

[5]*New York Times Book Review*, August 4, 1968, p. 24.

Southern Indo-China looked like Japan's last step before jumping off
for a full-scale attack in the Southwest Pacific. . . .

On the following day the President, receiving Nomura, proposed
that if the Japanese Government would withdraw its forces from
French Indo-China, he would seek to obtain a solemn declaration by
the United States, Britain, China, and The Netherlands to regard
Indo-China as a "neutralized" country, provided Japan gave similar
commitment. Japan's explanation for occupying Indo-China having
been that she wanted to defend her supplies of raw materials there,
the President's proposal took the props from under this specious rea-
soning. A week later the President extended his proposal to include
Thailand.

Indicating our reaction to Japan's latest act of imperialist aggression, the President froze Japanese assets in the United States on July
26. . . . All financial, import, and export transactions involving Japanese interests came under Government control, and thereafter trade
between the United States and Japan soon dwindled to comparatively
nothing. . . .

From now on, our major objective with regard to Japan was to give
ourselves more time to prepare our defenses. We were still ready—
and eager—to do everything possible toward keeping the United
States out of war; but it was our concurrent duty to concentrate on
trying to make the country ready to defend itself effectively in the
event of war being thrust upon us.[6]

It was, in fact, the movement by the Japanese from northern to
southern Indochina in July, 1941, and Roosevelt's reaction to it that
made war between Japan and the United States inevitable, despite
Roosevelt's deep desire to avoid a two-front conflict. The story con-
tinues down to the more familiar commitment in Southeast Asia,
from Truman to Nixon, to the less well-known fact that on four
separate occasions the Carter administration, in the wake of the
Communist takeover of South Vietnam in April, 1975, reaffirmed
the nation's treaty commitment to the defense of Thailand;[7] and, on
October 6, 1981, President Reagan said this to the prime minister
of Thailand on the occasion of his visit to Washington: "I can assure
you that America is ready to help you, and ASEAN, maintain your

[6]*The Memoirs of Cordell Hull* II (New York: Macmillan, 1948), pp. 1013–14.

[7]In the Carter administration those reaffirmations were made in May, 1978,
in Bangkok by Vice-President Mondale; in Washington in February, 1979, by President Carter; in July, 1979, in Bali by Secretary Vance; in June, 1980, in Washington
by Secretary Muskie.

independence against communist aggression. The Manila Pact, and its clarification in our bilateral communique of 1962, is a living monument. We will honor the obligations it conveys."[8]

That is where we are. With large Vietnamese forces in Kampuchea, just across the shallow Mekong from Thailand and dominating Laos as well: with the Soviet navy based in the installations we built in Cam Ranh Bay, the Soviet air force based in the airfields around Danang, and a major port in Kampuchea being enlarged for Soviet strategic purposes—just across the South China Sea from U.S. bases in Subic Bay and Clark Field—Southeast Asia is not likely soon to disappear from the national security agenda of the United States government. I doubt, however, that there is a wide awareness in the United States of how tightly drawn the confrontation is along the Mekong and across the South China Sea. Nor do I believe there is a wide awareness of the commitments reaffirmed in the region by President Carter and President Reagan. My point is this: We cannot understand what we have experienced in Asia over the past two generations, nor can we formulate and sustain a viable policy in Asia, until we as a nation come to a widespread understanding of the strategic importance of Southeast Asia to our own security and to the security of the other powers concerned.

I shall begin therefore by evoking the character of the strategic interests at work in Southeast Asia. Then I shall state the linkages of Vietnam to the rest of Southeast Asia, outline tersely the strategic evolution of Southeast Asia since 1940, and, finally, reflect on the implications of the story for U.S. policy—past and future.

The Strategic Interests of the Powers

At some risk of oversimplification, I shall try to define the major strategic interests of each of the principal powers concerned with Southeast Asia.

Japan. The Japanese have three abiding interests in Southeast Asia. First, a straightforward security interest that Southeast Asia

---

[8]The reference to the 'bilateral clarification' is to the Rusk-Thanat communique of March 6, 1962, which stated that the obligation of the United States in the event of aggression against Thailand ". . . does not depend on the prior agreement of all other Parties" to the Manila Pact.

NORTH AND SOUTH VIETNAM

CHINA

Red R.

Black R.

Dien Bien Phu

Hanoi

Haiphong

GULF
OF
TONKIN

Mekong R.

Luang Prabang

NORTH
VIETNAM

Vinh

HAINAN

L
A
O
S

Vientiane

DMZ

Con Thien
Quang Tri
Khe Sanh
Hue

THAILAND

Danang

My Lai

Khorat

Dak To
Kontum
Pleiku

Qui Nhon

Bangkok

CAMBODIA

CENTRAL
HIGHLANDS

Ban Me
Thuot

SOUTH

FISH
HOOK

Song Be
Loc Ninh

VIETNAM

CAM
RANH
BAY

Phnom
Penh

PARROTS
BEAK

An Loc

Bien Hoa

GULF OF SIAM

Saigon

IRON
TRIANGLE

Sihanoukville

Ca Mau

MEKONG DELTA

SOUTH CHINA SEA

0   100   200

Miles

SOUTHEAST ASIA

INDIA

CHINA

BURMA

TAIWAN

LAOS

Hainan

*PHILIPPINE
SEA*

NORTH VIETNAM

THAILAND

*SOUTH CHINA
SEA*

PHILIPPINES

CAMBODIA

SOUTH
VIETNAM

*GULF
OF
THAILAND*

M A L A Y S I A

Mindanao

*CELEBES
SEA*

Sumatra

Borneo

Celebes

*INDIAN
OCEAN*

I N D O N E S I A

JAVA • SEA

Java

Portuguese
Timor

0 100 200 300 400

Miles

(and thus the South China Sea) not be controlled by a potentially hostile power, with all that would imply for the sea approaches to the Japanese islands. Second, trading access to the countries of Southeast Asia that have been and remain major sources of raw materials and major markets for Japanese exports, markets notably expanding in recent decades. Third, an interest that the Strait of Malacca remain reliably open for Japanese trade with the rest of the world, an interest greatly heightened by the remarkable emergence of Japan as a global trading nation and its heavy reliance on an unobstructed flow of Middle East oil.

Japan sought to achieve these objectives by creating the Greater East Asia Co-Prosperity Sphere in 1940–45. When that effort failed, it fell back to reliance on the United States (and, to a degree, its own diplomacy and defense forces) to assure these vital interests.

China. China has an abiding interest that Southeast Asia not be dominated by a major, potentially hostile power. Such dominance would threaten it both overland and via the South China Sea, where Vietnamese bases could bring pressure against important coastal cities. China has pursued these interests since 1949 by contesting vigorously Soviet efforts to dominate Southeast Asian Communist parties, notably the Vietnamese; by leading the 1964–65 effort to collapse non-Communist resistance in Southeast Asia, in association with Hanoi and Sukarno and Aidit in Indonesia; and, after the Cultural Revolution, by association with the United States and by contesting independently what the Chinese regard as Soviet efforts to encircle and isolate China.

U.S.S.R. Russia has had an abiding interest that Vladivostok remain open as a trading port and a naval base. And, since the Trans-Siberian railway went through in the 1890s, it has been a recurrent contestant for power in northeast Asia, notably vis-à-vis Japan and China. In the post–1949 period, the Soviet Union moved out from this regional role to broader vistas of Asian and global power. Its contest for power developed two new dimensions: the struggle with the Chinese Communists, initially confined to contention for leadership of Asian (and other) Communist parties, which, from early 1958, became a cold war between the two countries; and the thrust, based on the radically expanded Soviet navy, to develop a string of alliances from Southeast Asia through the Indian Ocean to the Arabian Peninsula and East Africa. (I shall have more to say later about this policy, which can be formally dated from June, 1969.) The Soviet air and naval bases in Indochina are, evidently, fundamental to this strategy both to neutralize the U.S. bases at Clark Field and Subic Bay, which have hitherto dominated the South China Sea, and to guarantee Soviet access to the Indian Ocean through the Strait of Malacca.

India. Aside from an Indian Ocean open freely to its commerce and not dominated by a single potentially hostile power, India's concern with Southeast Asia is that the countries of the region— Burma, above all—remain independent. It is an interesting parallel, for example, to India's concern for an independent Afghanistan—a concern only recently articulated by Mrs. Gandhi.

India's interest in Southeast Asia is rarely discussed in public by its political leaders. Nevertheless, the fundamental strands of Indian policy toward the region have been consistent and deeply rooted in memories of the Japanese occupation of Burma and the possibility of a recurrence of danger on India's northeastern frontier.[9] For this reason, India supported Burma and Malaya against Communist guerrilla movements in the 1950s.

Australia. The abiding interests of Australia in Southeast Asia are dual: that its sea routes to the United States, Europe, and Japan (now its most important trading partner) remain open; and that Southeast Asia—above all, Indonesia—remain independent of any major power and not hostile. The Australians are not likely to forget what a close thing it was in 1942 when they were saved from Japanese invasion by the American victories in the Coral Sea and at Guadalcanal. Unlike most Americans, they remember how close to a Communist takeover Southeast Asia was, including, especially, Indonesia, in July, 1965, when Johnson made his decision to introduce large U.S. forces into Vietnam.[10]

In the changing circumstances since 1965, Australian foreign

[9]India's policy towards Southeast Asia is traced down to 1960 in Ton That Thien, *India and Southeast Asia, 1947–1960* (Geneva: Librairie Droz, 1963).

[10]See Howard Beale, *This Inch of Time* (Melbourne: Melbourne University Press, 1977), pp. 168–69. Beale, Australian ambassador to Washington in the 1960s, explains why Australia in 1956 joined in the effort to save South Vietnam.

and military policy has continued steadily to support the independence of Southeast Asia.

The United States. U.S. policy in Asia began, of course, with a
simple concern for the maintenance of trading access in the face of
special interests developed by Western powers operating in the region. From, say, the ambiguities of the Open Door notes of 1900
and Theodore Roosevelt's tilt towards the Russians in 1905 at Ports-
mouth, in the wake of the Russo-Japanese war, a strategic dimension to U.S. policy emerged parallel to the one that emerged during World War I in Europe; namely, a U.S. interest that a balance
of power be maintained in Asia and that no single power dominate
the region. A power with hegemony in Asia would command the
resources to expel U.S. naval power in the Pacific, back to Hawaii,
at least, just as a hegemonic power in Europe could dominate the
Atlantic, as German submarines twice came close to demonstrat-
ing. The United States has acted systematically on that principle for
some eighty years when the balance of power in Asia seemed in
real and present danger. At various times, that instinctive policy
has brought us into confrontation in Asia with Japan, China, Russia
or their surrogates; and, at various times, it has brought us into
association with Russia, China, and Japan.

As is evident from this brisk review, Southeast Asia is a critical
element in the balance of power in Asia because of its relation to
sea routes and the exercise of sea and air power; its resources; and
its location with respect to China, India, and Japan. For the United
States, Southeast Asia has a quite special meaning as an area of
forward defense of the Pacific—a relationship vividly demonstrated
after the loss of the Philippines to Japan in 1942. But for victory in
the battle of Midway, we might, at best, have held Hawaii.

In addition, the United States shares to a significant degree the
specific interests in Southeast Asia of its allies and others whose
security would be threatened by the hegemony of a single power
in Asia—that is, at the moment we share to a significant degree the
interests of Japan, China, India, and Australia as outlined earlier. It
is essentially a negative interest satisfied, as all the presidents from
Roosevelt to Reagan have stated, by an independent, neutral
Southeast Asia.

Southeast Asia. Southeast Asia, excluding the three states of

Indochina, contains some three hundred million people—a population approximating that of Latin America or Africa. They are diverse in their racial origins, historical experiences, degrees of modernization, and forms of government. History has also given them territorial and other deeply rooted conflicts to overcome. What they share is a desire to modernize their societies in their own way—true to their own cultures, traditions, and ambitions—and to be left in peace and independence by all the external powers. They do not wish to be run from Tokyo or Washington, New Delhi or Beijing, Moscow or Hanoi. In the 1960s and 1970s they also shared an astonishing economic and social momentum, including a per capita growth rate in real income averaging about 4 percent and a manufacturing growth rate of about 10 percent, as well as high rates of increase in foreign trade. They export about 83 percent of the world's natural rubber; 80 percent of its copra, palm, and coconut oil; and 73 percent of its tin, as well a wide range of other agricultural products and raw materials. Their literacy rates, which ranged from 39 percent to 72 percent in 1960 now range from 60 percent to 84 percent.

Out of their several and collective experiences as objects of the strategic interests of others, strongly encouraged by Lyndon Johnson who made Asian regionalism a major, consistent theme of his policy, and conscious that the U.S. role in Asia was likely to diminish with the passage of time, the five Southeast Asian countries (beyond Indochina) created the Association of Southeast Asian Nations (ASEAN) in 1967. It is an organization committed to economic and technical cooperation, to the peaceful settlement of its internal disputes, and, above all, to ensuring the stability and security of member countries "from external interference in any form or manifestation."[11] ASEAN moved forward slowly, building up the habit of economic cooperation and political consultation.

When the Communists took over Vietnam in April, 1975, ASEAN, alarmed by the turn of events, moved forward rather than backward. At a historic, carefully prepared session of the chiefs of government at Bali, in February, 1976, they strongly reaffirmed a

---

[11]See Association of Southeast Asian Nations, *10 Years ASEAN*, compiled and edited by the ASEAN secretariat under the direction of Secretary-General Umarjadi Njotowijono (Djakarta, 1978), p. 14. The quotations from the preamble to the founding Bangkok Declaration, signed August 7, 1967.

1971 declaration calling for a zone of peace, freedom, and neutrality in Southeast Asia. They have subsequently sought widened international support for this objective. Quite specifically, they have led the international effort to achieve the withdrawal of Vietnamese troops from Kampuchea and fostered the negotiation of a new national coalition of Kampuchean leaders committed to the authentic independence of their country. Although the countries of ASEAN command, neither individually nor collectively, the military power to deter or defeat a Vietnamese thrust into Thailand or to assure control over the critical sea lanes that surround them and link them to each other, the sturdy unity they have managed to maintain for fifteen years makes ASEAN an element in the Asian equation of diplomacy to be reckoned with.[12]

To sum up this review of various strategic perspectives on Southeast Asia, one can assert two propositions: (1) the legitimate interests of all the powers concerned with the region would be satisfied by a neutral Southeast Asia left to develop in independence, with its sea lanes and strategic straits open by international consensus, but (2) the fundamental character of their various interests at stake in the region decree that the effort of any one power to achieve dominance in the region will confront serious and determined opposition from multiple directions.

Vietnam and Southeast Asia

As the agenda of this symposium and the bulk of the literature bearing on these themes suggest, Vietnam has tended to be discussed by Americans without reference to Southeast Asia as a whole. None of the nine presidents caught up in the era thought in

[12]The confidence and strength built up in ASEAN between 1967 and 1975 by its continued high rate of economic and social progress, combined with the increased solidarity of the organization, contributed to an important result expressed in 1981 by the Malaysian foreign minister. (Keynote address by H. E. Tan Sri M. Ghazali Shafie, "ASEAN: Contributor to Stability and Development," at the conference "ASEAN: Today and Tomorrow" [Fletcher School of Law and Diplomacy, Boston, November 11, 1981], 15.) "In 1975 North Vietnamese tanks rolled past Danang, Cam Ranh Bay and Ton Son Nut into Saigon. The United States withdrew their last soldiers from Vietnam, and the worst of ASEAN's fears which underscored the Bangkok Declaration of 1967 came to pass. But ASEAN by then had seven solid years of living in neighbourly cooperation. Call it foresight, or what you will, the fact remains that with ASEAN solidarity there were no falling dominoes

such terms, not even Nixon who was the most reticent about articulating the importance of the region and the U.S. interest in its fate.

Rather than taking Vietnam's strategic importance for granted as part of Southeast Asia, it is worth briefly specifying both its intrinsic importance and the nature of its linkages to Southeast Asia.

First, its geography places it on the Chinese frontier; its ports and air bases make it of strategic importance with respect to both South China and the international sea lanes of the South China Sea. Thus the Soviet naval and air bases in Cam Ranh Bay and Danang are a serious concern, indeed, for China, Japan, the United States, every country in non-Communist Southeast Asia, and every country with an interest in the independence of Southeast Asia.

Second, easy overland access from Vietnam to Laos and Cambodia made it likely that those with power in all of Vietnam would quickly gain control of all of Indochina. The likelihood is enhanced by the extremely difficult logistical problems for an outside power (for example, the United States or China) of bringing its forces to bear in defense of Laos or Cambodia against an overland thrust from Vietnam. Control of Cambodia by an outside power substantially enhances the capacity of that power to bring air and naval forces to bear across the air and sea lanes of the South China Sea. For example, the destruction of the British battleship *Prince of Wales* and the battle cruiser *Repulse*, critical for the defense of Singapore, was accomplished by Japanese bombers in December, 1941, based on a hastily constructed airfield in Cambodia.

Third, for American policy in the 1950s and 1960s, a power emplaced in Vietnam, Laos, and Cambodia confronts Thailand across the long line of the shallow Mekong. The frontier is not only long and virtually indefensible against a massive attack by well-armed conventional forces, but the Mekong is also a long way from the Thai ports. As I have explained at length elsewhere, this is why John Kennedy in 1961 made the decision to defend Thailand and the rest of Southeast Asia by seeking to neutralize Laos by diplomacy and by fighting the battle for Southeast Asia in Vietnam.[13]

---

in Southeast Asia following the fall of Saigon to the Communists, and the United States withdrawal from Southeast Asia."

[13]W. W. Rostow, *The Diffusion of Power* (New York: Macmillan 1972), pp. 265–72.

Thailand is, ultimately, critical to Southeast Asia because of its geographical relation to Burma, on the one hand, Malaysia and Singapore, on the other. If a single major power controls all of Indochina and Thailand, the vital interests of India, Japan, the United States, Indonesia, and Australia are in real and present danger—that is, control over Burma and the land route to the Indian subcontinent; control over the South China Sea; and control over the Strait of Malacca. That is why Carter and Reagan have reaffirmed the applicability of our treaty commitments to Thailand and why the major political thrust of ASEAN, overwhelmingly backed by North and South in the United Nations, is to effect the withdrawal of Vietnamese forces from Kampuchea and the line of the Mekong and to create an authentically independent Kampuchean government.

Four Efforts at Hegemony

As Franklin Roosevelt suggested to the Japanese ambassador in July, 1941, a neutral Southeast Asia, of the kind ASEAN now proclaims, would satisfy the legitimate interests of all the powers; but he could not accept Japanese control over the region. Roosevelt's policy has, in effect, been the policy of all his successors. And the fact is that for more than forty years now a succession of powers has sought hegemony in the region and met serious resistance.

This sequence of efforts is reflected in the analysis I have thus far presented. But it may be useful briefly to specify when and the context in which each occurred.

First, of course, was the Japanese thrust of 1940–45. Its frustration required a maverick and bloody effort by the United States, Australia, New Zealand, Great Britain, China, and India.

Second, systematic Communist efforts were made to exploit by guerrilla warfare the postwar dishevelment of the region and the confusions and conflicts of the transition from colonialism to independence. Stalin organized this campaign, anticipating that the Communists would emerge victorious from the post–1945 civil war and that Truman would launch a counterattack against Soviet aggression in Europe. The Truman Doctrine and Marshall Plan of 1947 clearly set a limit to the ample European empire Stalin acquired in the wake of World War II.

But with Mao evidently on his way to control over China in 1947, ambitious new Communist objectives in Asia were enunciated by Zhdanov at the founding meeting of the Cominform in September. Open guerrilla warfare began in Indochina as early as November, 1946, in Burma in April, 1948, in Malaya in June of that year, and in Indonesia and the Philippines in the autumn. The Indian and Japanese Communist parties, with less scope for guerrilla action, nevertheless sharply increased their militancy in 1948. As a final victory was won in China in November 1949, Mao's political-military strategy was openly commended by the Cominform to the Communist parties in those areas where guerrilla operations were under way. Stalin and Mao met early in 1950 and confirmed the ambitious Asian strategy, planning its climax in the form of the North Korean invasion of South Korea, which took place at the end of June, 1950.

The American and United Nations response to the invasion of South Korea, the landings of Inchon, the March to the Yalu, the Chinese Communist entrance into the war, and the successful UN defense against a massive Chinese assault in April and May 1951 at the thirty-eighth parallel, brought this phase of military and quasi-military Communist effort throughout Asia to a gradual end. Neither Moscow nor Peking was willing to undertake all-out war or even accept the cost of a continued Korean offensive. And elsewhere, the bright Communist hopes of 1946–47 had dimmed. Nowhere in Asia was Mao's success repeated. Indonesia, Burma, and the Philippines largely overcame their guerrillas. At great cost to Britain, the Malayan guerrillas were contained and driven back. Only in Indochina, where French colonialism offered a seedbed as fruitful as postwar China, was there real Communist momentum. The settlement at Geneva in 1954 permitted an interval of four years of relative quiet in Indochina.

Although there were latent tensions between Moscow and Beijing in this phase and some contest over control and influence of the various Asian Communist parties, by and large the USSR and China conducted this second effort to achieve hegemony in Asia in concert.

The third effort emerged at a meeting in November, 1957, in Moscow in the wake of the Soviet launching of Sputnik in October.

The chiefs of all the Communist governments assembled. They agreed the time was propitious for a concerted effort to expand Soviet power. As Mao said in Moscow:

> It is my opinion that the international situation has now reached a new turning point. There are two winds in the world today, the East wind and the West wind. There is a Chinese saying, "Either the East wind prevails over the West wind or the West wind prevails over the East wind." It is characteristic of the situation today, I believe, that the East wind is prevailing over the West wind. That is to say, the forces of socialism are overwhelmingly superior to the forces of imperialism. . . .
>
> The superiority of the anti-imperialist forces over the imperialist forces . . . has expressed itself in even more concentrated form and reached unprecedented heights with the Soviet Union's launching of the artificial satellites. . . . That is why we say that this is a new turning point in the international situation. . . .[14]

Many enterprises followed from this assessment of "the new turning point," from Berlin to the Congo to the Caribbean. For the purposes of this paper, the most important was Soviet and Chinese agreement to permit Ho Chi Minh, under pressure from the Communists in South Vietnam, to relaunch Hanoi's effort to take over Laos and South Vietnam by guerrilla warfare after four years of relative passivity.

The spirit at Moscow was relatively harmonious between Russia and China; but by early 1958 the split, long latent, became acute over the question of the degree of control Moscow would exercise over the nuclear weapons it promised to transfer to China.[15] From that time forward, the competition for influence in Hanoi between Moscow and Beijing, long a major issue, became intense.

Until 1965 the Chinese influence was by and large predominant. Hanoi's enterprise, notably its introduction of regular North Vietnamese units into South Vietnam in 1964, was orchestrated by the Chinese, with the Indonesian confrontation with Malaysia. Sukarno left the United Nations and openly joined with the Chinese, North Vietnamese, Cambodians, and North Koreans in a new

---

[14]Quoted in John Gittings, *Survey of the Sino-Soviet Dispute, 1963–1967* (London: Oxford University Press, 1968), p. 82.

[15]For analysis of this critical turning point in modern history, see my *Diffusion of Power*, pp. 29–35.

grouping of forces as Hanoi's efforts in South Vietnam moved forward towards apparent success. On January 1, 1965, Chinese Foreign Minister Chen Yi proclaimed: "Thailand is next." No leader in Asia, Communist or non-Communist, doubted the potential reality of the domino theory in July, 1965, when Johnson made his decision to introduce substantial U.S. forces into the region. (This was the ominous setting Ambassador Beale evokes in his explanation of why Australia joined in the American effort; see below, note 10.)

The U.S. move was followed by the joint Communist effort, acquiesced in by Sukarno, to assassinate the Indonesian chiefs of staff and set up a Communist government. It failed. And, for related but obscure reasons, Mao's Cultural Revolution began in China a few weeks later. The Russians took over the major role in Hanoi of arms supplier and economic support, a position they still occupy.

The fourth and current thrust for hegemony in Southeast Asia is Brezhnev's, to which we have already referred. From the trough in 1965, the South Vietnamese moved forward slowly but consistently over the next two years in military, political, and economic terms. In the face of their waning position, the North Vietnamese and the Vietcong assembled their accumulated capital and threw it into a maximum effort at Tet 1968. The result was a major military and political victory for the South Vietnamese, a major political victory for Hanoi in American public opinion.[16] With Nixon's decision for Vietnamization, based on a more confident position in Vietnam, Moscow proceeded to design and announce a new, ambitious long-run policy.

The policy was explained by Brezhnev to a group of Communist leaders on June 7, 1969.[17] His plan was based explicitly on the "vacuum" left by the British withdrawal east of the Suez, the expected U.S. retraction in Asia reflected in Nixon's Guam Doctrine, and alleged Chinese efforts to expand into the vacuum. Implicitly, it was based on the greatly expanded capabilities of the Soviet Navy

[16]For a detailed analysis of this episode, see my *Diffusion of Power*, pp. 438–503.

[17]Brezhnev's speech and its strategic implications were well reported in a despatch from Moscow in the *New York Times*, June 13, 1969, pp. 1, 5.

generated during the 1960s and planned for the future. It also constituted a response to Nixon's interest in an opening to China.

The plan called for a new collective security for Asia; that is, a series of pacts with countries in Asia, the Middle East, and Africa, including Soviet bases in the periphery from the South China Seas to the western coasts of the Indian Ocean and the Persian Gulf. Over the next decade this policy, systematically pursued, included as major moves: the setting up of Soviet bases in Indochina and support for the Vietnamese invasion of Kampuchea; the 1971 Soviet pact with India; the creation of new Soviet ties to Yemen and Ethiopia; and, indeed, the Soviet occupation of Afghanistan. The policy is reflected in the number of Soviet operational ship visits in the Indian Ocean—they rise from one in 1968 to an average of 120 in the period 1974–76.[18]

The outcome of Brezhnev's Soviet-led collective security system for Asia, in the great arc from Vladivostok to Aden and Djibouti, is evidently still to be determined.

Some Reflections

Before considering the future prospects of the region and U.S. policy towards it, we might reflect a bit on the meaning of the analysis I have presented.

Perhaps the first thing to be said is that, while Americans may still debate the importance of Southeast Asia to the balance of power in Asia, as a whole there is little ambiguity about the matter among the governments and peoples of Asia, including the Soviet Union.

As for us Americans, some may draw from the story I have sketched the simple conclusion that all nine of our presidents since 1940 have been wrong; that is, the United States has no serious legitimate interests in preventing the control of Southeast Asia by a major, potentially hostile power. In that case, they should advo-

[18]Richard B. Remnek, "Soviet Policy in the Horn of Africa: The Decision to Intervene," in Robert H. Donaldson (ed.), *The Soviet Union in the Third World: Successes and Failures* (Boulder, Colo.: Westview Press, 1981), p. 130.

cate the abrogation of the network of commitments we have in the region and urge us to organize urgently to face all the profound military, diplomatic, and economic consequences that would flow from that decision.

If we assume that I have described more or less accurately the interests of all parties at stake in Southeast Asia, the sequence of events since 1940, and where the region now stands, there are a few reasonably objective observations to be made that bear on the central purpose of this symposium, which is to provide a perspective on our travail over Vietnam.

First, the nature of U.S. interest in Southeast Asia is quite complex—more so in Vietnam itself; and even when U.S. interests are less complex, we have had difficulty acting on them in a forehanded way. When the chips were down in 1917—with the German declaration of unrestricted submarine warfare in the Atlantic and the Zimmerman note promising the return of Texas to Mexico by a victorious Germany—it was not difficult for Wilson to gain congressional support for a declaration of war in a hitherto deeply divided country, only five months after he was reelected on the slogans "He kept us out of war" and "Too proud to fight." But such critical circumstances were required to bring the country to act on the basis of a wide consensus. Similarly, it required Pearl Harbor to bring the United States into World War II after a long period dominated by an isolationism Roosevelt couldn't break. And it took a straightforward invasion of South Korea to evoke a military response there. What Truman and Eisenhower, Kennedy and Johnson were trying to prevent in Southeast Asia was a circumstance so stark and dangerous that once again, late in the day, the American people would finally perceive vital interests were in jeopardy and be plunged into major war.

Behind their efforts was a consciousness that there has been, historically, no stable consensus in our country in the nature of our vital interests in the world. We have oscillated between isolationism, indifference, wishful thinking and complacency, on the one hand, and, on the other, the panic-stricken retrieval of situations already advanced in dangerous deterioration. We have operated systematically on the principle enunciated by Dr. Samuel Johnson: "Depend upon it, Sir, when a man knows he is to be hanged in a fortnight, it concentrates his mind wonderfully." Right or wrong, Kennedy and Johnson did not doubt that the American people and the Congress would react to support the use of force if Communist forces were actually engulfing all of Southeast Asia; but they judged a typical, late convulsive American reaction—a fortnight from the gallows—too dangerous in a nuclear age.

This was Kennedy's understanding of his position late in 1961:

> Before deciding American power and influence had to be used to save Southeast Asia, Kennedy asked himself, and put sharply to others, the question: What would happen if we let Southeast Asia go? Kennedy's working style was to probe and question a great many people while keeping his own counsel and making the specific decisions the day required. Only this one time do I recall his articulating the ultimate reasoning behind the positions at which he arrived. It was after the Taylor mission, shortly before I left the White House for the State Department.
>
> He began with domestic political life. He said if we walked away from Southeast Asia, the communist takeover would produce a debate in the United States more acute than that over the loss of China. Unlike Truman with China or Eisenhower in 1954, he would be violating a treaty commitment to the area. The upshot would be a rise and convergence of left- and right-wing isolationism that would affect commitments in Europe as well as in Asia. Loss of confidence in the United States would be worldwide. Under these circumstances, Krushchev and Mao could not refrain from acting to exploit the apparent shift in the balance of power. If Burma fell, Chinese power would be on the Indian frontier: the stability of all of Asia, not merely Southeast Asia, was involved. When the communist leaders had moved—after they were committed—the United States would then react. We would come plunging back to retrieve the situation. And a much more dangerous crisis would result, quite possibly a nuclear crisis.[19]

Johnson stated a similar proposition in an address at San Antonio on September 29, 1967:

> I cannot tell you tonight as your President—with certainty—that a Communist conquest of South Vietnam would be followd by a Communist conquest of Southeast Asia. But I do know there are North Vietnamese troops in Laos. I do know that there are North Vietnamese trained guerrillas tonight in northeast Thailand. I do know that

---

[19]Rostow, *Diffusion of Power*, p. 270.

there are Communist-supported guerrilla forces operating in Burma. And a Communist coup was barely averted in Indonesia, the fifth largest nation in the world.

So your American President cannot tell you—with certainty—that a Southeast Asia dominated by Communist power would bring a third world war much closer to terrible reality. One could hope that this would not be.

But all that we have learned in this tragic century suggests to me that it would be so. As President of the United States, I am not prepared to gamble on the chance that it is not so."[20]

Second, and quite specifically, Kennedy and Johnson fought in Vietnam to prevent the situation we now confront and what may (but may not) follow from it; that is, large Vietnamese forces on the line of the Mekong backed by a major hostile power. Historians, as well as American citizens, will no doubt assess their judgment on

---

[20]*Public Papers* (Washington, D.C.: Government Printing Office, 1968), p.488. And, retrospectively, Johnson wrote in *The Vantage Point* (New York: Holt, Rinehart, and Winston, 1971), pp. 152–53:

". . . Knowing what I did of the policies and actions of Moscow and Peking, I was as sure as a man could be that if we did not live up to our commitment in Southeast Asia and elsewhere, they would move to exploit the disarray in the United States and in the alliances of the Free World. They might move independently or they might move together. But move they would—whether through nuclear blackmail, through subversion, with regular armed forces, or in some other manner. As nearly as one can be certain of anything, I knew they could not resist the opportunity to expand their control into the vacuum of power we would leave behind us.

"Finally, as we faced the implications of what we had done as a nation, I was sure the United States would not then passively submit to the consequences. With Moscow and Peking and perhaps others moving forward, we would return to a world role to prevent their full takeover of Europe, Asia, and the Middle East— *after* they had committed themselves.

". . . My generation had lived through the change from American isolationism to collective security in 1940–1941. I had watched firsthand in Congress as we swerved in 1946–1947 from the unilateral dismantling of our armed forces to President Truman's effort to protect Western Europe. I could never forget the withdrawal of our forces from South Korea and then our immediate reaction to the Communist aggression of June 1950.

"As I looked ahead, I could see us repeating the same sharp reversal once again in Asia, or elsewhere—but this time in a nuclear world with all the dangers and possible horrors that go with it. Above all else, I did not want to lead this nation and the world into nuclear war.

"This was the private estimate that brought me to the hard decision of July 1965."

this matter in different ways. What I am asserting is that U.S. policy in the 1960s cannot be understood without grasping this dimension in the perspectives of Kennedy and Johnson.

A third objective observation is that, within the American foreign policy establishment of the 1960s—including some in the executive branch—there was a kind of geological fault line between those who regarded the balance of power in Southeast Asia as important for the United States in itself and those who, holding what I have called an Atlanticist view, regarded the maintenance of our commitments there as significant only for the viability of our commitments elsewhere; for example, in Europe and the Middle East.[21] The hypothesis of Gelb and Betts, stated at the beginning of this paper, reflects, for example, the latter view. In the early 1970s, having gathered strength for some time, a version of that view became widespread: that the costs of holding the U.S. position in Southeast Asia were excessive, even though our ground forces were withdrawn by 1972 and our air and naval forces in 1973. The view was not always expressed in the colorful terms quoted earlier from John Galbraith and Eugene McCarthy; but it was there.

From the perspective of the 1980s, I would only observe that the view that Southeast Asia doesn't much matter may have diminished somewhat with the emergence of ASEAN and the remarkable expansion in the economies of its members, including sophisticated trade and financial relations with the United States. They may not have yet achieved the respectability of Japan, in the eyes of Atlanticists, but they are clearly beyond the water-buffalo stage and on their way.

A fourth observation arises from the fixation current in the quarter-century after 1949 that China was the ultimate threat to Southeast Asia. I suspect, but cannot prove, that one element in the extraordinary performance of the American Congress towards Vietnam in the period 1973–75 may have been the belief that, with Nixon's new opening to China, the strategic threat to Southeast Asia had been once and for all lifted and therefore the aid promised

---

[21]For an analysis of this difference in perspective, see, for example, *Diffusion of Power*, pp. 492–97.

by Nixon to Thieu could be ruthlessly reduced. The possibility of the Soviet Union replacing China as a threat in the region, not difficult to deduce from Brezhnev's collective security plan of 1969, appears not to have been envisaged by Congress—and, perhaps, not by many in the executive branch.

So much for the complexities of interpreting the nature and extent of the nation's interest in the independence of the countries of Southeast Asia. Now, what about the future? From one perspective, the Soviet position in the region—and Brezhnev's 1969 plan as a whole—does not, at the moment, appear on the verge of success. The movements of Soviet naval and air forces around the region constitute a significant psychological pressure and political presence; but, for the time being, one would not expect a decisive Soviet thrust to dominate the region like that of Japan in 1941 and 1942. The Soviet Union confronts a considerable array of problems that render this an apparently unpropitious time for great adventures: the costly stalemate in Afghanistan; India's taking its distance from Moscow on Afghanistan, despite the 1971 treaty; the state of Poland and all its multiple implications for the Soviet security structure; deep and degenerating problems within the Soviet economy. Similarly, the presence of the Vietnamese forces on the Thai frontier are a source of great anxiety, indeed, to all the non-Communist governments of the region and China; but Hanoi appears to have quite enough trouble in South Vietnam, in Kampuchea itself, and in trying to achieve an economic revival at home without plunging into a wider Southeast Asian war. Besides, it has been reminded forcefully that Chinese forces are on its northern frontier.

No doubt there are those who will say: Some but not all the dominoes have fallen; life goes on in most of Southeast Asia; what is there to worry about? But two facts should be remembered. First, the Communists, unlike ourselves, are patient, persevering, and stubborn in pursuing their long-run strategies; and, second, there is no power capable of preventing the Soviet Union from dominating Southeast Asia—indeed, all of Asia—except the United States. Asia would promptly become a quite different place if the United States closed down Clark Field and Subic Bay, pulled the Pacific Fleet back to Hawaii, and announced that the guarantees to Thailand were no longer operative.

In short, despite the debacle of 1975, the possibility of an independent, neutral Southeast Asia—so important for so many, including the 300 million men, women, and children who live there—has not been lost. But it will not be held without a deep and steady understanding in the United States of the stakes involved—an understanding notably lacking in our nation in the intense domestic debate of the period 1965–75 and in the subsequent literature on the subject.

As a coda to this analysis, I would only add that, beyond our time, in the next century, the peace of Asia is likely to depend on a solemn agreement between India and China that they should both support Southeast Asia in its desire for independence, thus creating a buffer that might avoid the two countries repeating in Asia the tragedy of France and Germany in Europe.

Aspects of the Vietnam Legacy

ROBERT BLY

The Erosion of Male Confidence

MY subject is the erosion of male confidence in general during the last thirty years, and, specifically, the part the Vietnam War has had in that erosion. Everywhere I go in the country I meet men roughly twenty to forty years old who live in considerable self-doubt. Many of them have few or no close male friends. I meet young fathers who do not know what male values they should attempt to teach their sons. These men, often separated from their own remote fathers, and out of touch with their grandfathers, do not feel they belong to a community of men. When they reach out toward truly masculine values, they find nothing in their hand when it closes.

The old anger against the father, so characteristic of the nineteenth century and earlier centuries, has been replaced in many men by a kind of passivity and remoteness, which springs from a feeling that the father has abandoned or rejected them. In some cases, the father lost his sons in divorce proceedings, and many sons interpret that event to mean that men are untrustworthy. Still other sons have lived with remote, overworked, impassive, silent, controlling or condemnatory fathers; and one feels in these men a longing for male values mingled with a kind of helpless bitterness. Some men in recent years admire only certain values which they associate with women—tenderness, concern for the environment, nurturing, the sense of cooperation, ability to feel deeply. These men characteristically confide during a crisis only in women. That is fine; what is missing is the confiding in men. We could conclude by saying that women came out of the sixties and seventies with considerable confidence in their values, but men lack this clarity and belief. We all know many exceptions to this statement, and yet we sense a significant alteration in male confidence since, say, 1950 to 1960.

Because men of all social classes have lost confidence, it's clear that many forces affect this change. The Industrial Revolution has sent the father to work many miles from the home, and given him a work that he cannot teach his son. Male societies have disappeared, along with opportunities for older and younger men to meet each other and to do ordinary physical work together. The mythological layer, with all its models of adult male energy—Apollo, Dionysius, Hermes, Zeus—collapsed long ago, as have models of adult female energy for women. More recently, the relatively humane, or humanized, male battle disappeared, destroyed by machine-gun slaughter and bombing from the air. In old Irish and Greek stories we meet men who obey the rules of combat and honor their male enemy.

We all notice that suburban life gets along without male community. My parents brought me up on a Minnesota farm during years in which men lived in a community. My father ran a threshing rig, and all through the threshing season the men—young, old, and middle-aged—worked together, doggedly and humorously, in a kind of high-spirited cooperation at its best. I felt a confidence in the male community and I felt the goodness of it. But for men living in the suburbs all that is gone. We can all suggest many other forces and events that have contributed to erosion of male confidence. I would say that the two major causes for erosion are the attacks launched against men by the separatist part of the women's movement and the Vietnam War.

The women's movement has brought considerable psychic health to women, but we need to distinguish the women's movement from its separatist component: the attacks that heap together virtually all male values and condemn them as evil, and that locate the source of women's pain entirely in men. At a seminar three days ago a woman said to me, "Since all good poetry comes from our reaction to oppression, and since white males are not oppressed in any way, then how could they possibly write poetry?" So I asked, "Does your mother oppress you?" "Oh, not at all," she said. "Women don't oppress, men oppress." So I said, "How do you feel about the matriarchies?" She said, "Oh, there was no oppression in the matriarchies." I said, "Read Margaret Mead sometime." Some feminists are determined to save men even if they have to destroy them to do it.

An ancient story from north England about the ugly dragon man called the Lindworm says that the transformation of the Lindworm to a man takes place in four stages. The Lindworm's "bride," rather than fighting the Lindworm, asks him to take off one of his seven ugly skins, and she agrees to take off one of her seven blouses if he does that. After he has removed all seven skins, he lies helpless and white on the floor. She then whips him with whips dipped in lye, then washes him in milk, and finally lies down in the bed and holds him a few minutes before falling asleep. Connie Martin, the storyteller, has suggested that women in the seventies got the whipping part down well, but did not wash the man or hold him. They were too tired after the whipping to do the last two steps.

Let's turn now to the Vietnam War and its influence on men's confidence. That subject is what concerns us here. To introduce the subject, I'll tell two stories that I heard. A friend in Boston told me the first story. He stems from an old and wealthy family that carries a lot of military tradition and so much emphasis on male values that even civilians in his family receive a sort of military burial, with only the men present. My friend, whom I will call John, entered, as one would expect, the military service during the Vietnam War willingly, trustingly—became an officer and served in the field. After some duty in the field, he returned to Saigon on leave. One day he found himself by the river talking to an old captain, both of them speaking French. The Vietnamese river captain told him, in the course of many anecdotes, that the American soldiers were not welcome here, any more than the French. John had experienced inconsistencies in the field, but at that instant he felt a terrific shock. He understood that he had been lied to. The men who had lied to him were the very men that his family had respected for generations—military men and men in responsible government positions. Last night we saw a section of the new PBS documentary of the war. In that section one can watch McNamara and McGeorge Bundy lying about the Tonkin Gulf incident. I said to John, "What did you do then when you realized that you had been lied to about

the major issues of the war?" "Well," he said, "a strange thing happened. A female anger rose up in me." I said, "Why do you use the
word 'female'?" He said, "All at once I understood how a single
betrayal could bring a woman to furious anger. The Greeks talked
about that. I understood that female anger, and I felt it." I said,
"What happened next?" He said, "Well, the anger continued and
turned into rage and I had to live with that the rest of the time I
was in Vietnam, and I'm still living with it." He is a friend of John
Kerry, who organized the Vietnam Veterans against the War. He
remarked that John Kerry has entered politics in Massachusetts—
holds a high office—and Kerry still has a nightmare every night.
Not one night goes by that he does not have it.

I know anecdotes don't prove anything; they only suggest. To
me they suggest that a new situation evolved during the Vietnam
War which amounts to older men lying to younger men. This is the
grief I want to discuss.

I enlisted in the Second World War when I was seventeen and
I, like most of the men I knew, did not feel that older men lied to
me during the war. The older men, I felt, were aware of the
younger ones, and though many younger men died, the older men
died as well. There was a certain feeling of camaraderie and trust
all up and down the line. My friend John emphasized that the military and civilian leaders this time did not labor to awaken the sense
of patriotism that gives battle labor some meaning. That sense of
meaning bound old and young together in the Second World War.
Johnson didn't declare war because to do so would have necessi-
tated a full congressional debate. Did you see Dean Rusk lie about
that point last night in the documentary? He said, "Well, we didn't
try to declare war because, you see, we were afraid that it would
be, you know, you mustn't when you have nuclear arms, you
mustn't make people angry." Dean Rusk was lying. As the Vietnam
War went on, Walt Whitman Rostow, McGeorge Bundy, Dean
Rusk, all lied. And I felt lied to by them. But at the time, I didn't
fully realize how the soldiers and officers in the battlefield would
feel when, their lives at stake, they recognized the same lies.

I will tell a second story. I met recently in San Francisco a
veteran who had been an ordinary draftee. When I told him I
would be attending a conference in Texas about the war, he looked

interested, and I asked him how he felt now about the war. He said, "Well, I must tell you that I still feel tremendous anger." I said, "What about?" "Well," he said, "I've been thinking about it, and it has to do with my background. At the time I was a young Catholic boy from Pennsylvania. I had taken in certain moral values, simply through being in that background. One was that killing was wrong. A second was respect for women. We even believed some of the moral declarations that racism was bad. All at once we were out in the jungle, and told to shoot at anything that moves. We couldn't tell if the people we were killing were men or women, let alone Communists or peasants. Moreover, everyone, officers included, called them 'slopes' and 'gooks.' The older men never mentioned this nor told us what we were to do with the ideas we had taken in during Catholic grade school. After a month or so in the field suddenly I was shipped for R and R to a whorehouse in Thailand. Something was wrong with that. A lot of us still had feelings toward women. We had feelings about respect for women and what a woman means this way. Something got broken in me, and I'm still angry about that."

So the question we have to ask ourselves is, Who made that decision? I remember that during the Second World War the army supported the USO, where one went and danced a little with a woman, who was equally shy. It was very square, but nevertheless, the whole thing helped to preserve some continuity between civilian life and war life. Older men like Eisenhower supported such arrangements. The older men in the Vietnam War led the way to the whorehouses and made no attempt to preserve the continuity between civilian life and war life for these young males. It was a violation of trust. To repeat: when I came out of the Second World War there was a bond between younger and older men and it helped all of us who served to move through our lives.

Let's turn now to body counts. The army didn't announce body counts of Germans during the Second World War. As a speaker mentioned yesterday, we measured our progress in Vietnam not by land taken but by lives taken. "Attrition" is the sugar-coated way of putting it. But the fact is that counting dead bodies is not a way for civilized human beings to behave, especially when your culture emphasizes the dignity of life. How can the same culture that prides itself on respecting the dignity of human life be in favor of body counts? The counting of bodies and the release of that information daily was approved by the Joint Chiefs of Staff, and agreed on by the generals. You can't tell me that they didn't know the implications of this. Even worse, the generals and the Pentagon began to lie about the number of bodies. As we now know, the staff often doubled the count from the field. General Shoemaker, who led the incursion into Cambodia, is present, and several speakers have addressed polite questions to him during their talks here. I'd like to ask him a question also. General Shoemaker, I would like to ask you now: "Were you aware of the false body counts being passed through you?"

"Yes, I was aware that some of them were inflated."

"Have you apologized to the young men in the country for this lie?"

"Well, I would prefer to listen to you."

"All right. Thank you."

You heard the answer General Shoemaker just gave us, "No, I have not apologized to the young men in the country." And we can add that he doesn't intend to.

Our subject here is the bad judgment of older men that resulted in damage to younger men or death of younger men. John mentioned one more decision. The generals decided to have a 365-day field term rotation. Such a plan broke with the traditional situation in which a company lives and dies together as a unit. The company learns to act as a unit; and each man learns to trust, or whom to trust. But the 365-day rotation breaks all that. Everyone is thinking, as John mentioned, about his own survival, and then suddenly the others can't depend on him, or he on them. I think the average age of the soldiers in Vietnam was around eighteen years old; in the Second War World it was around twenty-six. The average age of the company commanders in Vietnam was twenty-two years old; in the Second World War, thirty-six. The decision for rotation was a bad one, and I think General Westmoreland made it; others here would know. General Westmoreland throughout did many stupid things, and his advisors showed a specialist mentality, and a massive insensitivity to the needs of the younger men. The use of Agent Orange is a perfect example. Our first step in recovering from the war, I think, is simply to say this.

So the eighteen-year-olds were out in the jungle with men only two or three years older, and these eighteen-year-olds felt completely isolated and separated. Who made the decisions that led to this isolation? Did everyone approve of the public body counts? I will recite to you a poem I wrote in the spring of 1966 about those body counts. It's called "Counting Small-Boned Bodies."

Let's count the bodies over again.

If we could only make the bodies smaller,
The size of skulls, maybe we could get
A whole plain white with skulls in the moonlight!

If we could only make the bodies smaller,
Maybe we could get a whole year's kill
In front of us on a desk!

If we could only make the bodies smaller,
Maybe we could fit a body
Into a finger ring, for a keepsake forever.

I always thought that we never made good enough use of the Vietnamese heads. Maybe the Pentagon should have encased them in plastic and put them up on motel walls around the United States. Couldn't American men and women make love well below those heads?

Walt Rostow made a remark this morning which you all heard. I don't want to single him out above the others of his sort—it happens he is the only one here representing that group of advisors, and it is brave of him to come. But I could hardly believe my ears this morning when he declared that the true brutality in this war was the brutality of Congress when it refused to vote more money toward the end. Did you hear that one? It was marvelous. Our feelings get damaged when we misuse our own language. All through the war, men like Rostow refused to use language in a clear and honest way. "Brutality" comes from the root, "brute"; and "not voting funds" comes from a decision based on rationality and debate. Words and phrases like "friendlies," "incursion," "Communist infrastructure," and "strategic hamlets" testify to a time in American history when language failed. And it was the older men who brought in that language, and led the movement toward failure of language. They had the responsibility to keep the language clear. The young men can't do that. They are helpless. They believe the older men when they called a dictatorship "democratic," or when they called a certain liquid "Agent Orange" rather than "Poison no. 465." Doesn't "Orange" imply nourishing?

We can say then that when the Vietnam veteran arrived home he found a large hole in himself where his values once were. What is the veteran going to do about that? Many veterans I meet say they still cannot find any values to put in there. The earlier values were blown out, the way acid blows out the brain. Harry Wilmer moved me tremendously when he talked about the dreams of Vietnam veterans yesterday. The dreams of certain veterans, he said, repeat events in exact detail, endlessly, meaninglessly. Only when the veteran is able to find a possibility of meaning—what a wonderful word that is—meaning, meaning, meaning—can his dreams begin to change. Then a veteran can begin to put something into this hole. But most veterans are not receiving help in moving toward meaning; they have not succeeded in finding a man like Harry Wilmer. They live in rage and in a sense of betrayal.

It is clear that this issue is a very serious issue, and the implications go far beyond the mistakes of the Vietnam War. When men lose their confidence in older men, what happens then? When older men betray younger men, and lie to them, in government and in the field, what happens then to male values? What happens to a society in which the males do not trust each other? What kind of a society is that? Do you feel it coming now? That mood in the country? Do you feel how the distrust erodes the confidence that males have in themselves? Did you know that the practice of "fragging," that is the killing by enlisted men of their own sergeants and lieutenants, was statistically not a factor until the Vietnam War? And I feel the poison of that distrust moving through the whole society now. The older men associated with the Vietnam War continue to lie to Vietnam veterans about chemical poisoning, and birth defects. Every man in the country knows that. It is no wonder that in Comtrex advertisements on television men are always presented as weak. What does the army's constant lying about Agent Orange do to our respect for men and for male values?

Our general subject is the Vietnam War and its effect on the erosion of male confidence. How can this nightmare end? What healing can take place? Harry Wilmer suggests, and I utterly agree, that no healing can take place until we decide to take in the concept of the dark side, or the shadow. Each of us has a dark side. If I shout at my small sons, I can say that I have a fatherly duty to discipline them, but we know that this shouting has a dark side. When so many whites moved to the suburbs during the fifties, wasn't that a simple longing for open space? But it had a dark side. The dark side was that we let the centers of our cities disintegrate, in the same way that we let the center of our psyche disintegrate. When entertainment, in the form of television, floods our house every night, we are only sitting and listening—this is a simple thing surely, isn't it? But it has a dark side. It has a very strong dark side, in that we don't have to entertain others, or enter any larger sort of community to be entertained. Why don't we ever talk about that one? Well, when Johnson decided to raise troop levels sneakily, without public debate, that looked like a simple act, perfectly reasonable under the circumstances, as Dean Rusk says. But we know that it had a dark side. The decision to send eighteen-year-olds to whorehouses, whether they wanted to go or not, has a dark side, and the cool dryness with which Robert McNamara and McGeorge Bundy and Dean Rusk discussed hideous realities has a dark side. Have you ever noticed that? How calm the older men are? Some rationalists don't want to get into feeling at all. Did you notice how boyish McNamara looked in the documentary last night? I was shocked. Probably he looked that way because he was a boy. What is a boy? A boy is a person who takes an act and does not think about the dark side of it. An adult is a person who takes an act and remains aware of its dark side. What happens in the psyche when Reagan repeats over and over that we fight our wars with noble purpose while the other side fights its wars with evil purpose? What happens when we say that Russia is an "evil empire"?

Some Europeans studied the dark side of colonial wars, and Joseph Conrad studies it marvelously in his story, *The Heart of Darkness.* We have to think of the possibility that we are adopting European diplomatic phrases and adopting European global responsibilities, but adopting them not as adults but as boys. When we decisively entered Vietnam culture around 1966, we had virtually no one in the State Department who spoke Vietnamese, and very few in the academic community who had close knowledge of Vietnamese culture. Do you think that deterred our people? Not a bit. We invaded a nation and made decisions for it when we had only two or three scholars who could speak the language. That is not adult behavior. Our behavior in Central America is not adult behavior either. Reagan is another boy, an aged boy. How to embalm a boy so he always smiles forever? How could we be so lucky as to find a president who never sees the dark side of anything he does? These boyish men—so cheerful—are among the most dangerous men on earth. One group of Americans carries the knowledge of their danger: the Vietnam veterans. They carry that knowledge for all of us.

I am going to read now some sections of a poem I wrote during the Vietnam War called "The Teeth Mother Naked at Last." I don't want to read this poem. During the last ten years or so various people have asked me to read the poem in public and I have said no, I'm not going to read it. I don't like to read it any more. I don't want to read it. But since one purpose of this conference is to dip down into that old water, I will read some of the poem here. It tries to say how the war felt—not to a poet, just to a human being. I will start with the first section.

Massive engines lift beautifully from the deck.
Wings appear over the trees, wings with eight hundred rivets.

Engines burning a thousand gallons of gasoline a minute sweep
    over the huts with dirt floors.

The chickens feel the new fear deep in the pits of their beaks.
Buddah with Padma Sambhava.

Meanwhile, out on the China Sea,
immense gray bodies are floating,
born in Roanoke,
the ocean on both sides expanding, "buoyed on the dense marine."

Helicopters flutter overhead. The death-
bee is coming. Super Sabres
like knots of neurotic energy sweep
around and return.
This is Hamilton's triumph.
This is the advantage of a centralized bank.
B-52s come from Guam. All the teachers
die in flames. The hopes of Tolstoy fall asleep in the ant heap.
Do not ask for mercy.

Now the time comes to look into the past-tunnels,
the hours given and taken in school,
the scuffles in coatrooms,
foam leaps from his nostrils,
now we come to the scum you take from the mouths of the dead,
now we sit beside the dying, and hold their hands, there is
        hardly time for good-bye,
the staff sergeant from North Carolina is dying—you hold his
        hand,
he knows the mansions of the dead are empty, he has an empty
        place
inside him, created one night when his parents came home drunk,
he uses half his skin to cover it,
as you try to protect a balloon from sharp objects. . . .

Artillery shells explode. Napalm canisters roll end over end.
800 steel pellets fly through the vegetable walls.
The six-hour infant puts his fists instinctively to his eyes to
        keep out the light.
but the room explodes,
the children explode.
Blood leaps on the vegetable walls.

Yes, I know, blood leaps on the walls—
Don't cry at that—

Do you cry at the wind pouring out of Canada?
Do you cry at the reeds shaken at the edge of the sloughs?
The Marine battalion enters.
This happens when the seasons change,
This happens when the leaves begin to drop from the trees too
    early
"Kill them: I don't want to see anything moving."
This happens when the ice begins to show its teeth in the ponds
This happens when the heavy layers of lake water
    press down on the
    fish's head, and send him deeper, where his tail swirls
    slowly, and his brain passes him pictures of heavy reeds, of
    vegetation fallen on vegetation. . . .
Hamilton saw all this in detail:
"Every banana tree slashed, every cooking utensil smashed, every
    mattress cut."

Now the Marine knives sweep around like sharp-edged jets; how
    beautifully
    they slash open the rice bags,
the mattresses. . . .
ducks are killed with $150 shotguns.

Old women watch the soldiers as they move.

    II

Excellent Roman knives slip along the ribs.

A Stronger man starts to jerk up the strips of flesh.

"Let's hear it again, you believe in the Father, the Son, and the
    Holy Ghost?"

A long scream unrolls.

More.

*"From the political point of view, democratic institutions are
    being built in Vietnam, wouldn't you agree?"*

A green parrot shudders under the fingernails.
Blood jumps in the pocket.
The scream lashes like a tail.

*"Let us not be deterred from our task by the voices of
    dissent. . . ."*

The whines of the jets
pierce like a long needle.

As soon as the President finishes his press conference, black
    wings carry off the words,
bits of flesh still clinging to them.

       *   *   *

The ministers lie, the professors lie, the television lies, the
    priests lie. . . .
These lies mean that the country wants to die.
Lie after lie starts out into the prairie grass,
like enormous caravans of Conestoga wagons. . . .

And a long desire for death flows out, guiding the enormous
    caravans from beneath,
stringing together the vague and foolish words.
It is a desire to eat death,
to gobble it down,
to rush on it like a cobra with mouth open

It's a desire to take death inside,
to feel it burning inside, pushing out velvety hairs,
like a clothes brush in the intestines—

This is the thrill that leads the President on to lie

       *   *   *

Now the Chief Executive enters; the press conference begins:
First the President lies about the date the Appalachian Mountains
      rose.
Then he lies about the population of Chicago, then he lies about
      the weight of the adult eagle, then about the acreage of the
      Everglades

He lies about the number of fish taken every year in the Arctic,
      he has private information about which city *is* the capital of
      Wyoming, he lies about the birthplace of Attila the Hun.

He lies about the composition of the amniotic fluid, and he insists
      that Luther was never a German, and that only the
      Protestants sold indulgences,

That Pope Leo X *wanted* to reform the church, but the "liberal
      elements" prevented him,
that the Peasants' War was fomented by Italians from the North.

And the Attorney General lies about the time the sun sets.

      Do you want me to stop this? Do you feel depressed? Good. I
want you to listen to these next lines. I believe that the way the
older men lie implies self-destruction. Older men do not betray
younger men with the consistent betrayal that happened in the
Vietnam War unless there is something deeply disturbed way down
inside.

These lies mean that we have a longing to die that we do not
      recognize.
It is the longing for someone to come and take you by the hand to
      where they all are sleeping:
where the Egyptian pharaohs are asleep, and your own mother,
and all those disappeared children, who used to go around with
      you in the rings at grade school. . . .

Do not be angry at the President—he is longing to take in
      his hand
the locks of death hair—

to meet his own children dead, or unborn. . . .
He is drifting sideways toward the dusty places

III

This is what it's like for a rich country to make war
this is what it's like to bomb huts (afterwards described as
    "structures")
this is what it's like to kill marginal farmers (afterwards
    described as "Communists")

this is what it's like to watch the altimeter needle going mad

*Baron 25, this is 81. Are there any friendlies in the area? 81 from
25, negative on the friendlies. I'd like you to take out as many
structures as possible located in those trees within 200 meters
east and west of my smoke mark.*

diving, the green earth swinging, cheeks hanging back, red pins
    blossoming ahead of us, 20-millimeter cannon fire, leveling
    off, rice fields shooting by like telephone poles, smoke
    rising, hut roofs loop up huge as landing fields, slugs going
    in, half the huts on fire, small figures running, palm trees
    burning, shooting past, up again; . . . blue sky . . . cloud
    mountains

This is what it's like to have a gross national product.

    I think I'll skip a little here.

This is what it's like to send firebombs down from air-conditioned
    cockpits.

This is what it's like to be told to fire into a reed hut with an
    automatic weapon.

It's because we have new packaging for smoked oysters that bomb
    holes appear in the rice paddies.

It is because we have so few women sobbing in back rooms,
because we have so few children's heads torn apart by high-
    velocity bullets,
because we have so few tears falling on our own hands
that the Super Sabre turns and screams down toward the earth.

It's because taxpayers move to the suburbs that we transfer
    populations.
The Marines use cigarette lighters to light the thatched roofs of
    huts
because so many Americans own their own homes.

IV

*   *   *

I know that books are tired of us.
I *know* they are chaining the Bible to chairs.
Books don't want to remain in the same room with us anymore.

New Testaments are escaping . . . dressed as women . . . they go
    off after dark.
And Plato! Plato . . . Plato wants to go backwards. . . .
He wants to hurry back up the river of time, so he can end as
    some blob of sea flesh rotting on an Australian beach.

V

Why are they dying? I have written this so many times.
They are dying because the President has opened a Bible again.
They are dying because gold deposits have been found among the
    Shoshoni Indians.

They are dying because money follows intellect!
And intellect is like a fan opening in the wind—

The Marines think that unless they die the rivers will not move.

They are dying so that the mountain shadows will continue to fall
    east in the afternoon,
so that the beetle can move along the ground near the fallen
    twigs.

One more small piece. I hate this section.

VI

But if one of those children came near that we have set on fire,
came toward you like a gray barn, walking,
you would howl like a wind tunnel in a hurricane,
you would tear at your shirt with blue hands,
you would drive over your own child's wagon trying to back up,
the pupils of your eyes would go wild—

If a child came by burning, you would dance on a lawn,
trying to leap into the air, digging into your cheeks,
you would ram your head against the wall of your bedroom
like a bull penned too long in his moody pen—

If one of those children came toward me with both hands
in the air, fire rising along both elbows,
I would suddenly go back to my animal brain,
I would drop on all fours screaming,
my vocal chords would turn blue, so would yours,
it would be two days before I could play with my own children
    again.

    I read parts of that poem, not because I wanted to, but because
if we are going to be healed we are going to have to go back into
what we did in Vietnam. The Germans after the Second World War
went into their actions and they didn't. They healed and they didn't
heal. Now, I think, if we are going to heal we have to take two
public acts. The first is public mourning. The American people
elected Carter and Reagan on a secret agreement that the two men
would never make us face the Vietnam War. But when we avoid
facing anything we get sick. When someone close to us dies, it is

important to mourn. A young man came up to me the other day and said, "I wanted to weep at my father's funeral, but I couldn't. What do you think about that?" We all get ill if we don't mourn. Lincoln was not a boy, and I believe that if Lincoln were president now the first thing he would do would be to call for a national day of mourning. He would say: "Please nobody go to work today. We are going to mourn for the Vietnam War today and mourn for the damage it has caused to us and to others. We are going to think about the rupture of faith between young and old men, and the rupture of faith between men and women." I think he would begin then with a deep cry, on national television—something like the old women who mourn at Greek funerals. Aaaaaaaahhhhhhhhh-aaaaaaaahhhhhhh. The sound would induce weeping. Lincoln might keep that up for a whole hour because he had the ability to mourn—as you can see by looking at his face.

Walt Rostow will soon give his major address and he will lie to us again in his cool dry way. There will be no grief in his voice. That doesn't bother me. What bothers me is that you, the audience, may comment and ask him questions in the same cool voice. What worries me is that, flattered by having a celebrity in the room, not one of you will say no to him.

The second public act I think essential is this: that the older men publicly apologize to the younger men. General Kinnard owes the younger men an apology in public, and I did feel some apology in the private talk he gave here yesterday. I think the Bundys should apologize. I think that McNamara should apologize. I hear that he had trouble sleeping after the war, but he has never talked about that in public. The young veterans now consider themselves crazy. The old men's apology and admission of their craziness could help bring the older and younger men together. I would say that extreme mourning in the service of human union is no vice.

I am going to leave the Vietnam War subject now and recite a recent poem that suggests the way I feel now. One of the gifts given as one gets older is being able to grieve more.

> What is sorrow for? It is a storehouse far
> in the north for wheat, barley, corn and tears.
> One steps to the door on a round stone.

The storehouse feeds all the kinds of sorrow.
And I say to myself: Will you have
sorrow at last? Go on, be cheerful in autumn;
be stoic, yes, be tranquil, calm,
or in the valley of sorrows spread your wings.

Philip L. Geyelin

The Vietnam Syndrome

Having chosen a cliché for a subject, I should probably define it. The dictionary says a syndrome is "a number of symptoms occurring together and characterizing a specific disease or condition." So the "Vietnam syndrome," presumably, is a general tendency to see in this or that situation conditions and characteristics that remind us of Vietnam. For many this is another way of saying that they remind us of something to be avoided at all costs. But the Vietnam War is not that easy to categorize. It was, obviously, not good. But neither was it in all respects bad. Ronald Reagan was not wrong when he called it a noble cause, if by that he meant that by and large good intentions paved the road to the roof of the U.S. embassy in Saigon in 1975. So what we have here is a collection of analogies, mostly subjective, that together constitute the Vietnam syndrome. The problem is how to distinguish between those Vietnam legacies—those effects on public opinion and on the performance of public officials, those conscious and unconscious reflexes—that inhibit useful undertakings, and those lessons that can put us on the right path, or steer us away from the wrong one. All of us can argue over which are good and which are bad. I shall discuss my own list and in the process offer my opinion of where we may suffer at the hands of the so-called Vietnam syndrome, and where we either have profited or might hope to profit from what we can learn from this tormenting chapter in United States history.

Damaging Legacies

I begin with those particular reflexes and responses to the Vietnam experience that lead in directions which are unconstructive and unlikely to contribute to effective public policy. I start with what appears to be a general debilitating and excessive distrust of government—of its policymakers, and of their policy. This distrust was compounded, of course, by Watergate. But Watergate was Son of Vietnam; it derived directly from Richard Nixon's desperate efforts to deal with the crippling impact of public dissent on his war effort. This was the first purpose of the "plumbers," the enemies list, the telephone taps, and all the rest—to strangle dissent. One cannot forget that line from a U.S. officer in Vietnam as he described to a group of reporters a village in ruins: "We had to destroy the village in order to save it." Watergate was Richard Nixon's way of saying that you had to destroy the American system in order to save it.

So we can trace to both Vietnam and Watergate what has clearly been a tendency to turn away in disillusionment from Washington and all things establishmentarian. We see it in the presidents we have elected since Vietnam—in a conscious or subconscious reaching out for candidates who have never been to Washington, except in the most casual way, people who for just that reason could have no clear connection one way or another with Vietnam. First we reached out to Plains, Georgia, and when we didn't like the results, we reached out to Beverly Hills.

Dean Acheson, the quintessential establishment man, was also a wise man, and he used to say that some awful fate condemned the United States to put people in the White House with no experience in foreign policy. Nixon was actually the most recent exception to that rule. Lyndon Johnson and Gerry Ford knew Washington, but even they did not claim a background or even much interest in foreign policy. Jimmy Carter and Ronald Reagan did not even know Washington. We find in their election some vestige of the Vietnam syndrome—some reflection of a public disillusionment with the performance of those who held office in the Vietnam years that has translated itself into a general distrust of almost anybody laying claim to past experience in statescraft.

The "Vietnam syndrome" syndrome is frequently found among those in policymaking or opinion-making positions today who supported the Vietnam War, who think our only failure was in not pursuing the war flat-out with whatever it took. This is a familiar political reflex—a "we were right the first time" cast of mind among those who cannot accept the possibility that the Vietnam War established limits on American power and ability to influence events. It shows itself in many ways, including a quick rush to judgment at the first bright flicker of jingoism in American public opinion. Iran, it was said at the time of the hostage crisis, was to be, in the words of William Hyland, a former senior member of Kissinger's national-security staff, a "watershed," for "it closes the Vietnam syndrome." But with Hyland, as with Zbigniew Brzezinski (who was saying the same thing privately as Jimmy Carter's national-security advisor), I suspect the wish was father to the thought.

But the wish was powerful and it still is. It found its loudest voice in the jungle yells of Al Haig at his confirmation hearings in the early days of the current administration. His "Me, Tarzan" approach to foreign policy is shared by Ronald Reagan and his associates and followers as well.

A recent *Dallas Times Herald* column mentions a speech by Thomas Reed, the number-three man in the National Security Council who, when making a speech, is making it on good authority. Reed argued that "there is nothing wrong with winning." People had likened him to Prime Minister Margaret Thatcher and Israel Defense Minister Ariel Sharon, he said, and he considered that to be "pretty good company." Now that is a terrible way to talk about a nice iron woman who did nothing more than blunder into a war and beat up the Argentines.

But even assuming that Margaret Thatcher likes the association with Sharon, I am not certain that he is the role model for which we are looking. Of these efforts to overcompensate for Vietnam losses, one can only say they are no less helpful to coherent and realistic foresight policy than the collapse of public confidence in government.

The flip side of "we were right the first time" is the quick conclusion that in just about every respect we were wrong. From this flows an instinctive reluctance to get involved, as they say on the street—to get involved even when a superpower like the United States has the same responsibility and obligation to get involved in certain circumstances as that of a citizen witnessing a crime.

The instinctive shying away from the threat of the use of force—from even the first hint of a potentially escalating entanglement—is as understandable as it is crippling to the pursuit of legitimate security interests. Much has been made of the way we got into Vietnam, of the landing of the first combat troops by Lyndon Johnson in March, 1965. We tend to forget that in April of that year Lyndon Johnson landed over ten thousand American troops a lot closer to home in the Dominican Republic. We also tend to forget that, as a consequence of their presence, Ellsworth Bunker, working for nearly a year, negotiated a settlement of that political conflict and that we have had two peaceful democratic transfers of government in the Dominican Republic since that time. That's one example of a careful combination of carrot and stick having a tremendously useful effect. Likewise, in 1958, when four different revolutions were underway in Lebanon, the U.S. Marines landed and within ten days Robert Murphy, a special envoy of the president, had negotiated an agreement that ended that crisis and gave Lebanon peace for at least another seventeen years.

This is really what the elusive and subtle concept of deterrence is all about. It can work. But to make it work, diplomacy has to be reinforced by the credible threat of the use of force. John Foster Dulles got himself into a lot of trouble talking about "the necessary art" of going to the brink. But no one complained when John F. Kennedy did it with arguable success in the Cuban missile crisis. One way to measure this aspect of the Vietnam syndrome is to ask what the public response would be today if the president of the United States suddenly deployed a naval blockade—an act of war—in a situation involving a comparable threat to U.S. security.

One can find some part of the answer in the initial reaction of Congress in 1982 to the very thought that U.S. Marines might be dispatched to Lebanon, this time in the company of French and Italian toops, for the strictly limited purpose of escorting Palestine Liberation Organization (PLO) militiamen out of Beirut. Right across the political spectrum, from Barry Goldwater to Ted Kennedy, the members of Congress rose up to demand what was going on. Kennedy said the safety of marines should be "guaranteed." Senator Richard Lugar, a conservative Republican, was "deeply concerned with any proposal that would put American military personnel in a situation where there is a strong likelihood they will be fired upon and would have to defend themselves." Senator Dodd, a liberal Democrat, said "I don't believe that you can achieve the kind of assurance that I would insist upon." Congressman Jim Leach said that is "a mistake of tragic proportions." These statements provide an interesting commentary on the mood of Congress—and its reading of public opinion. The president did not bow entirely to reaction—he merely assured the Congress that the United States Marines would be withdrawn "if they were shot at." I don't wish to play the warmonger, but the Middle East is surely central to U.S. security, and successful extraction of the PLO forces from Beirut and a peaceful end to the Lebanon war was surely in the national interest. It was vital that the United States be in a position to offer the services of its troops to that multinational force. The French and Italians were not holding back, yet the first reflex in Congress from the chairman of the House Foreign Affairs Committee was to raise serious questions about whether the president was about to violate the War Powers Resolution.

This brings me to the congressional Vietnam syndrome. It is reflected not only in the War Powers Resolution, which defined the conditions under which the president can commit American forces to a hostile environment, but also in the Clark Amendment, which says what we can and cannot do in Angola, and there is a general inclination for congressmen to elbow their way into the most intimate aspects of the conduct of diplomacy. Here we see a tendency to find in situations where there is a prospective U.S. military involvement those "symptoms and characteristics of a specific condition"—which is to say, the Vietnam War—where analogy doesn't apply. The practical effect of the congressional uproar over the marines in Lebanon is a good example. Under that pressure the administration was almost certainly too hasty in its removal of the marines from the scene. Reluctantly, resisting, the French and the Italians also left. Not long thereafter the Israelis sanctioned the entry of Christian militia forces into the refugee camps, Shatila and Sabra, with the horrible consequences familiar to all of us. You can't prove that this tragedy would have happened if the multinational force had remained, but it is a reasonable supposition. In any event, the inescapable conclusion was that the three-nation force had to return in the interest of shoring up the authority of the new Lebanese government.

And yet, in fairness, one has to put oneself in the place of a member of the Congress. The Tonkin resolution was shouted through the House and the Senate under the lash of President Johnson in 1964. Even those present members of Congress who were not there at the time remember that on that historic occasion the legislative branch was out for lunch. Only a brave few asked the right questions, and they were cut off by assurances from the floor manager of the bill in the Senate, William Fulbright, that the president had not the slightest intention of using that authority to land American troops for combat purposes in Vietnam.

But the resolution they so readily accepted became the legislative justification, regularly cited by Lyndon Johnson and Richard Nixon, for the policy of the United States in Vietnam for years to come. That is the stuff of which congressional syndromes are made. It is the stuff, I might add, of the congressional cut-off of military aid to South Vietnam in the middle of 1975. It is said that this lost the war for the South Vietnamese, and perhaps it did. It is also said that this aid cut-off violated a secret written agreement between Nixon and Thieu made in connection with the 1973 peace agreement.

But that is just the point; this was a *secret* commitment from Nixon—the fine invisible wire that held that flawed peace treaty together. It had to be a secret agreement because the president knew perfectly well what would happen if he had come before Congress and said that in order to make this agreement work we must commit ourselves, not only to continued military aid, but conceivably to a return to Vietnam as well. It was out of the question. It also reflected ignorance of the basic flaw in his own strategy—the limits imposed by the workings of an open society. Or perhaps it is contempt for the political process. As late as 1973, Secretary of Defense James Schlesinger was publicly threatening that we might have to return to Vietnam, so it wasn't just Nixon. Yet we could not conceivably have returned to Vietnam under the terms of congressional legislation then in effect. It was an utterly empty threat that could not possibly have deterred the North Vietnamese. For that matter, Nixon's secret letter to Thieu was certainly no way of deterring the North Vietnamese. I do not doubt a casual relation between what the Congress did and what the North Vietnamese then felt free to do, but one must consider the context in which Congress acted.

One cannot ignore the media Vietnam syndrome: once bitten, twice shy. There was a tendency to favor the government in the early days with a certain amount of trust—what the former director of the FBI, Patrick Gray, once described as "a presumption of regularity." It comes as no surprise that this presumption no longer exists. Here again, there is a syndrome at work, sometimes to excess, a tendency to assume the worst, to question everything, to seek out the soreheads in government and to give them a voice. This tendency on the part of those in the news business is complemented, I might add, by a genuine change in the attitude of those engaged in the policymaking process. Gen. Maxwell Taylor, the former ambassador to Saigon, took note of this in a recent article in the *Washington Post* on the missile crisis. He argued that "A President today cannot count on either the privacy or the loyalty that Kennedy enjoyed. He would be dangerously exposed to the vicious practice of leakage by government officials as a means of sabotaging the course of action of which they disapprove."

I don't know exactly how much of this to attribute to a Vietnam syndrome, but I think that the state of mind of policymakers is part and parcel of the collapse of confidence—the withholding of trust—that is evident with the public, Congress, and the press. It is an internal disintegration of discipline that has something to do with the fierce divisiveness engendered by Vietnam. It has something to do as well with an absence of the sort of collegiality at work in earlier administrations and better times. Part of this may well have to do with that turning away from professionals to amateurs, from the old-boy network of the eastern establishment to new players with no reverence for the older traditions. The difference is more quantitative than qualitative. Great issues of policy have always been aired by calculated leaks. But the new generation of journalists, and some who are old enough to have participated in the Vietnam experience, cannot forget that for a considerable period the media too easily accepted the government line and that an awful lot of the time the government line was misleading.

Where else do we find symptoms of this so-called syndrome? I suspect it is to be found in the resistance of nearly 500,000 young men in this country who this year [1982] defied the law requiring them to register for the draft. This is not like the 1960s protest. Over 90 percent of those eligible today have registered. But this action says something about a lingering antiwar, anti-military-service sentiment on the part of young people. It says even more when you consider that all they are being asked to do is to register; that we are almost alone, except for the British, among the nations of the North Atlantic Treaty Organization in not conscripting; that we are making do with a volunteer army that in no way reflects a cross-section of our society; that not even "the great communicator" with his ambitious plans for rapid deployment forces dares suggest that the burden of manning those forces be shared not just by those willing to volunteer their services, but by all eligible, able-bodied young men.

One can also include the nuclear-freeze movement as a product of what might be called the consciousness-raising effect of Vietnam. The nine nuclear-freeze propositions on the ballots in the congressional elections of 1982 did not escape the notice of Congress as it approached the defense budget.

The Vietnam syndrome cuts two ways. For some it has an inhibiting, restraining effect, for they see the war as a calamity, caused in large part by an overly ambitious, overly militant approach to the world. For others, Vietnam is merely an example of doing the right thing the wrong way and therefore an argument for a bigger, better-equipped U.S. defense force committed to act, not by graduated response in a limited war and creeping escalation, but by fighting to win. These entirely contradictory readings of Vietnam constitute the final negative element of the syndrome—continuing conflict and confusion over what the war was all about. The overhanging question marks are nowhere better illustrated than in the struggle in Washington over the design of the Vietnam Veterans Memorial. The struggle is a metaphor on the war itself.

The small group of veterans who started the project, led by Jan Scruggs, an ex-infantryman who was wounded in Vietnam, symbolized the extraordinary quality of those who call themselves "the survivors." They quarreled heatedly over the design and the very nature of the memorial, but they finally reconciled their differences in the way that precisely defines the two faces of the Vietnam syndrome. A young Yale University architectural student won the contest for the design of the memorial. Protest over the design's stark and muted statement quickly followed. It is a V-shaped black marble wall sunk below ground level, bearing the names of those who were killed. To this was added a rather more conventional monument—a statue of three members of the armed services and an American flag. It doesn't fit together aesthetically, yet it somehow strikes me as exactly the right way to solve an almost insoluble problem. It is a monument to dichotomy; in the form finally agreed on, it is an important statement. It invites, it nearly commands, a continuing questioning about Vietnam, a continuing quest for the right lessons. It commands us to regularly test our foreign policy against the Vietnam experience.

Positive Legacies

What I have outlined thus far has dealt with the least constructive aspects of this testing. But some legacies of the Vietnam War are positive and of great value, and I would put at the head of the list of such legacies the Vietnam veterans themselves. For the best part of a sabbatical year, I did research for a possible book on Vietnam veterans. They number 9 million, if we are talking about those who served in the Vietnam era; 2.7 million, if we are talking about those who served in the theater; and 1.6 million, if we are talking about those actively engaged in combat. In the course of dozens of interviews I reached one simple conclusion: there is no stereotype. And I made some friends.

Paul is a children's therapist in Buffalo, New York. He was badly wounded in Vietnam. He told me this story. He and five of his fellow soldiers stationed in Germany were sitting around one night arguing about Vietnam and whether they ought to go there. Five of the six eventually volunteered to go to Vietnam. Of those five, three were killed in action. One came home a double amputee. My friend Paul, after long rehabilitation, has been restored to health. He said that at least once a month he and the double amputee, who has a good job and a happy life in Philadelphia, get a call from the comrade who stayed in Germany. This man had had great success for a time as an advertising executive in Los Angeles, but he was guilt-ridden and became an alcoholic. When I tried to reach him in California, he was in a detoxification program.

One cannot neatly categorize the victims; they run a wide gamut. Bob Muller, the head of the Vietnam Veterans of America, was shot in the chest leading a charge up a hill as a captain in the Marine Corps. He is paralyzed from the waist down, but he and his wheelchair have been in every corner of this country trying to build his organization.

Dean Phillips is a young lawyer in the Veterans Administration. He was a highly decorated paratrooper in Vietnam as a noncommissioned officer. He developed, in the course of his career, a certain irreverence for authority. When they tried to give him his second Silver Star he contrived—I can't imagine how—to roar by the reviewing stand in a jeep at the very moment when he was supposed to be arriving for the ceremony, and "mooned" the assembled officers on the stand. He later joined Vietnam Veterans against the War and threw his medals over the fence in the Washington protest march. He is now wearing a three-piece suit at the Veterans Administration. But, more important, Dean is disturbed in a different way. He worries about our foreign policy. At the time of the Iranian crisis, he volunteered for the reserves. He went down to Fort Bragg. He took the training, and he went back to jumping. I asked him why he was putting himself through all of this and he said that while he was on duty in the reserves the enlisted men he saw in the volunteer army reminded him of the Vietnam draftees; young, disproportionately minority-group members and high-school dropouts. He said if they were ever going to be sent to another war, he wanted to be with them.

Angel Palmadino is the director of the Veterans Outreach Center in Manhattan. I met him at a conference under the auspices of an organization called World without War. There were veterans, journalists, and some very establishment poeple in the audience, such as William Bundy and Ellsworth Bunker. After a good deal of discussion, Angel took the floor. He is a short, chunky Chicano with black hair down to his waist. As he spoke he did a kind of whirling-dervish dance around the room, waving his arms, and shouting. He talked about the troubled veterans he meets at the outreach center, "young guys who went to fight a war when they were eighteen and didn't know what they were doing" and got screwed. But he went on to speak of the generation of Vietnam veterans, now in their thirties, some of them lawyers, doctors, and in the upper echelons of American society. "So it is not a question of America coming around to us, no, no, no," Angel said. "Patriotism," he said, "we got it . . . we are men . . . and a lot of us are hurting bad . . . but we are going to save each other . . . America, if you want to be a part of it, come on. If you don't, look out—because we are going to set some policies in the future. . . . The sixties generation is the hope of America and I am the cream of the crop and you remember that when you leave this stinking room." He concluded: "If there is going to be another war, I am going to tell my sons that they are going to go when I decide. But it had better be a good war. In fact, if it's that good, I am going."

That's Angel. It's also not a bad summation of the human legacy of Vietnam that is likely to play an increasingly powerful and positive role in the social and political scene. Besides the human legacy, another positive development coming out of the Vietnam War—perhaps the most important one—is an acute awareness that was not there in the Vietnam years of the need to consider, in making foreign policy, the consent of the governed. I have spoken to the excesses of oversight by Congress. I am talking now of the necessity for a reasonable degree of public debate and public support.

It is interesting that this lesson is one which McGeorge Bundy has himself accepted. In his days as the president's national security advisor in the White House he was a model of secrecy and discretion when a journalist wanted to know what was going on. But never mind, in a speech nine years ago talking about American policy in the Middle East, Bundy was critical of precisely the kind of governmental noncommunication that characterized the conduct of the Vietnam War. Cryptic press conferences and back-channel conversations with journalists will no longer do the job, he said. A lot needs to be said, and no policy that requires public support can be sustained without such exposition.

But if that is what Bundy is preaching as a professor now, he is touching on a critical point. For this is not just a fundamental constitutional principle—it is a matter of basic strategy. Vietnam has at least created, if not disposed of, the question of whether limited war, a whole new concept, can be effectively conducted in an open society. The awful irony here is that the intentions of these brightest and best that have been so put down were admirable. They designed what they thought was a way of keeping the war from expanding, of shortening it if possible, and avoiding the awful risk that Professor Rostow has spoken of—an escalation to the level of nuclear exchange. That was the theory of graduated response.

The other part of it was that the government had to make it believable to the people in Hanoi. It had to make them believe that they would go on forever, if it wanted them to stop way short. And that was where the policy collapsed—because that is a game of poker, a game of trying to drive the other guy out of the game. And for that, one needs a poker face. But a democracy cannot keep a poker face, and that is why Nixon needed the "plumbers."

There is other, more conspicuous evidence of a Vietnam syndrome usefully at work. At the beginning of the Reagan administration the plans for El Salvador invited a Vietnam analogy. We were going to increase military aid, we were increasing the number of advisors, we were training the El Salvador army in the fine arts of "search and destroy"—and they were using that term. There was every reason to suspect that the same progression that had taken place in Vietnam was beginning in El Salvador: American advisors, first staying in their camps, then going out on operations, then being armed, and then being authorized to shoot. The plan had escalation written all over it. But Congress moved in significantly with a Vietnam veteran, David Bonior, from Michigan, the leader of the twenty-member Vietnam caucus in the House. They insisted on an accounting of what was intended. They asked for information in advance—to know how far the administration wanted to go, what the terms were, and how human rights would be protected.

A Final Note

It is obvious that the Vietnam syndrome is a matter of opinion, is in the eye of the beholder. Some read the lessons in radical terms and others refuse to read them at all. But the lessons must be read with care and in a way that does not paralyze the necessary conduct of foreign policy in the interest of national security.

I would venture one further counsel. Reflections on the Vietnam experience concentrate logically and understandably on what actually happened. The effect in many instances is to lead people to the conclusion that the right thing now is to do exactly the opposite. We stare long and hard at the road that was taken, without perhaps addressing ourselves, to borrow from the title of a poem by Robert Frost, to "the road not taken," or, more precisely, to the several available roads not taken. Not all those roads would have led in exactly the opposite direction.

History is not too generous in its disclosure of alternatives, but one should note the principal purpose of collecting the Pentagon Papers, as explained to me by the man who ordered it, Secretary Robert McNamara. He said that future policymakers and historians could not possibly understand Vietnam without knowing not only why decisions went the way they did, and what alternatives were rejected, but also what was never even considered. For that purpose, you needed everything. You needed the comprehensive record. Sadly, the Pentagon Papers did not accomplish that mission. Because of a series of mishaps, the project took on a different form and was never completed. But McNamara was on the right track. In order to return to where we were before we got lost, it is important to search the lessons of Vietnam—to examine the thinking of the early 1960s. And, perhaps, to consider what Jack Kennedy was saying at that time.

I do not wish to invite an argument over whether President Kennedy would have pursued the same policy as Lyndon Johnson—surely he was as gung ho as anyone could have been in the early stages. He invented the Green Berets. But I would argue that toward the end, two months before he was assassinated, he was showing evidence of disenchantment. In September, 1963, he was saying there were limits on what the United States could do for any country. He was publicly critical of the Saigon government. "I don't think that unless a greater effort is made by the government to win popular support that the war can be won out there. In the final analysis it is their war and they are the ones who have to win it or lose it. We can help them, we can give them equipment, we can send our men out there as advisors, but they have to win it, the people of Vietnam against the Communists." You can read a lot or a little into that, but on its face it suggests an alternative that wasn't chosen.

Undoubtedly, we can find as many different lessons in the Vietnam experience as there are different poeple participating in this symposium. We cannot hope to fully understand the Vietnam War, or even to agree about it, through a weekend symposium. We may not understand it for years. But on one point I think we all agree: We owe it to those who have sacrificed themselves in good faith, believing with good reason in the rightness of their sacrifice, to try to understand it.

Harry A. Wilmer

War Nightmares: A Decade after Vietnam

In 1835 de Toqueville wrote in *Democracy in America* that "in times when the passions are beginning to take charge of the conduct of human affairs, one should pay less attention to what men of experience and common sense are thinking than to what is preoccupying the imagination of dreamers."[1]

Today we live in perilous times. With international violence—war in the Middle East and Afghanistan, fighting in Central America, Africa, and the Caribbean—with American soldiers stationed in points throughout the world, with terrorism rampant, and violence almost accepted as a way of life, with unending terror in Northern Ireland, with starvation and poverty growing, with new missiles facing each other in Europe, with the nuclear threat growing in magnitude, and with the bodies of American soldiers coming back from overseas, we urgently need to understand the impact of war and violence on the human psyche.

This is a study of the unconscious impact of the war on the individual mind a decade after the American withdrawal from Vietnam. The psychological aftermath of the war, the catastrophic trauma upon civilians and soldiers, is revealed in the study of the stressful memories and nightmares of combat troops in Vietnam.

This paper presented at the Salado symposium was subsequently given as a plenary address at the Seventh International Transpersonal Conference at Devos, Switzerland, September 2, 1983, and as a lecture, December 2, 1983, sponsored by the C. G. Jung Institute of San Francisco. The ideas expressed are extensively reported in Wilmer's forthcoming book, *Dreams of Vietnam.*

[1] Alexis de Tocqueville, *Democracy in America*, ed. Richard Heffner (New York: Mentor Books, 1966).

Vietnam was a war where victory was measured not by territorial claims but by body counts, the relative number of dead corpses. It was a war that the United States fought for twelve years, and it was the first war that our nation lost.

I am not concerned with war atrocities themselves, but I know I must not turn away from these horrors before imparting some hope into an otherwise bleak picture. By confronting the darkness we can learn about the psychological nature of violence, or any catastrophe.

As a psychiatrist and psychoanalyst, I had an unusual opportunity to study the psychological trauma of the Vietnam War when I devoted two years to working with 103 Vietnam veterans at the Audie Murphy Veterans Hospital in San Antonio. During this time I studied the long-lasting psychological consequences of the Vietnam War revealed one decade after the end of the war. These veterans were men whose suffering had led them to seek help at the Veterans Administration (VA) hospital or the Veterans Center Outreach Program, and were referred to me. Some of the men have had psychiatric problems ever since they returned to the States; others began having nightmares years after they returned home.

Of these 103 men, 12 had no memory of dreams of Vietnam. I have no idea why they did not have, or remember, war dreams; but, given the experience of other veterans whose war nightmares did not begin until seven to ten years after the war, these men risk such dreams in the future. The remaining 91 veterans told me 359 dreams. Since I only counted the same nightmare once, the nightmares recurring week after week, month after month, year after year, totaled in the thousands.

One day five years ago, a Vietnam veteran told his nightmare to a dream seminar I directed for patients at the VA hospital. I was deeply moved and surprisingly affected by this group event because his nightmare, which had been recurrent several times a week for twelve years, was so vivid and so like the actual experience that each one of us in the group—patients and staff alike—felt as if he had been in Vietnam during this veteran's particular terror. This made me realize that I had been listening to Vietnam nightmares for years and had not really heard them. So I began to work with this veteran, whom I will call Jim, seeing him two or three times a week for three months and much less frequently for two years. Jim's dream reenacted—almost as if by camera verité or television—the time when he was point man leading seventeen soldiers to their deaths in an ambush in their first firefight.[2]

The dream relived the sudden panic—the men falling dead or screaming, wounded—of Jim's escape and his killing of a Vietcong in a foxhole where he hid just above the ravine while the VC executed each of the wounded men and then shot all the dead again and again, and Jim's horror as he held a grenade and froze. He couldn't throw it into the ravine until all of the men were killed because he would have killed his own men. Finally he threw it and he escaped back to the base camp. In the dream, as in real life, he returned to the ravine the next day with other soldiers to bring back the bodies. They had been decapitated and their heads put on punji sticks. Some of the bodies had been mutilated in other ways. After this experience, Jim broke down and was evacuated to the United States. He felt guilty, banished, rejected. He had been in and out of VA hospitals for years, maintained on medications. To handle his anger, fear, and grief, he drank excessively, became addicted to heroin, and smoked pot as often as he could. His extensive VA records contained no report of his nightmare and no details of his combat experience. I mention this because this was true of the records of almost all 103 veterans. When I asked Jim why he hadn't talked about his nightmare, his answer was characteristic of the problem. He said, "Nobody asked me."

After he had worked with me for about two months, his dreams began to change; at last the loop of repetitions was broken. In dream after dream Jim became each of the different persons in the nightmare: the executor, the executed. When his head was cut off with a sword, he ran after it as it rolled down a hill; he said he could see it with his soul that came out of his neck. He was with his psyche, which means "*soul.*"

Jim's dreams finally involved me as a wounded soldier in the ravine. With the help of a woman nurse to render first aid, he res-

[2]Harry A. Wilmer, "Vietnam and Madness, Dreams of Schizophrenic Patients," *Journal of the American Academy of Psychoanalysis* 10 (1982): 47–65; and James F. Veninga, "The Healing Nightmare: A Conversation with Harry Wilmer," *Texas Humanist* 5, no. 2, November-December, 1982): 3–5.

cued me and carried me back to the base: he had saved the wounded healer with the aid of his feminine side. His dream of rescuing me continued until one night, instead of waking up sweating and frightened, he woke up for the first time crying. This was the turning point, when his grief and mourning began the healing process. Within a few months his nightmares began to wane until they finally became a relatively minor problem for him.

If Jim's nightmares were clues to his healing, could the dreams of the other veterans facilitate their healing process? The literature was little help. Combat nightmares have been known to be the hallmark of what was called "shell shock" in World War I, "battle fatigue" or "war neurosis" in World War II, and "post-trauma stress disorder" since 1979.[3] War nightmares are a unique form of dreams. Freud despaired of them because they were an exception to his theoretical formulations. Jung was so pessimistic about them in his writings that he felt one would have to wait to let them stop of their own accord. However, one of his closest colleagues in Zurich, Marie-Louis von Franz, told me recently that Jung successfully treated a British World War II soldier suffering from war nightmares, and that Jung arrived at a symbolic understanding similar to what I have found. Our similarity in approach demonstrates the truth of Goethe's aphorism, "Everything has been thought of before, the difficulty is to think it again."

So frightening are the war nightmares that veterans are usually reluctant to talk about them to anyone. The American people wanted to forget Vietnam. The veterans and their nightmares were, and continue to be, grim and terrible reminders of what happened to enormous numbers of men, and some women too, although there were no women referred to in my study. These nightmares are symbolic of our national nightmare that would not go away, and will not go away until we face it, hear it, see it; then, we can go on, stronger because of our facing that defeat, that tragedy. It has been estimated that at least 500,000 out of the 2.9 million soldiers sent to Vietnam now suffer psychologically and need help.

I explained to each man who came to see me that I would meet

---

[3]Harry A. Wilmer, "Post Traumatic Stress Disorder," *Psychiatric Annals* 12 (1982): 995–1003.

with him for two or three hours on two or three days and would tape-record our interviews for the purpose of a study to be published in a book. Each veteran signed an informed consent. With many veterans I supplemented the three hours with brief psychotherapy, when long-suppressed hurts and memories surfaced to crises in the initial meetings. For example, some of these men, believing they were still in Vietnam, had awakened from their nightmares choking their wives. I videotaped sessions every six months to document the changes in two cases. My observations were not a part of their clinical records, and in no way did my opinions affect their chance of receiving compensation: I was simply on sabbatical in the VA hospital, doing a special study to help understand the Vietnam veteran.

Except on rare occasions, when my judgment told me that I was hearing "war stories" or an unusual embellishment, distortion, or falsification, I took what each veteran told me as his truth. I use the phrase "his truth" not derogatorily, but to indicate an authentic individual perspective. In a few instances I might have been deceived; but to seek corroborative data, to talk with "informants," as we say in medical and psychiatric history, to check details would have cast a pall over my study and destroyed a trust which developed between these veterans and me. I say this not because it was part of my plan to verify their memories, but because such a study naturally arouses such questions. The characteristic war nightmare as recalled is exactly like the real event. How precisely it mirrors external reality is not the important point. The details of any real event are modified by different observers—as the Rashomon effect indicates; with dreams the dreamer's perception of its proximity to real events is the most important consideration.

The dream images are perhaps our only living uncontaminated record of the war trauma. They are what lies beyond the silence and are testimony to the failure of words, even of reason; and they symbolize the disastrous impotence of our sacred technology, our overwhelming war machines, our power and wealth and pride that could not prevail against the spirit and determination of guerilla fighters in a tiny nation.

I have been describing the nightmares as replicas of the reality.

I found that these kinds of dreams constituted 47 percent of the war dreams, repeating the same horror night after night. Relentless and predictable, at first these did not seem like dreams at all, but the stuff of which dreams are fashioned. In time, however, I came to see these spectres of reality as the archetypal dreams of war. The characteristic war dreams were expressions of actual circumstances that human beings are subjected to, where there can be no basis for metaphorical transformation because the reality image itself is the most powerful expression of the feelings involved. There is no antecedent human resource that can molify the intensity of the images. Such archetypal dreams are both symbol and metaphor at the same time.

I have divided war dreams into four classes. First, the dream of the actual event, *the actual dream* (47%). Second is *the possible dream* in which something else had been added to the real events, something that did not occur but could have happened. The possible dream begins the creative scenario of the dream world's healing process. Dreams in this category account for 17 percent of the Vietnam dreams, as in the following example: Patient dreams he has thrown a Vietcong prisoner out of a helicopter—something he did not actually do but which he had heard of others doing.

The third category is *the improbable dream* (12%), which is metaphorical: only by the wildest stretch of the imagination could it have occurred, as in this example: Patient dreams he sees a helicopter crash. The pilot walks toward the dreamer, but just as they come face to face the dreamer sees that the pilot is unscathed; at that moment the dreamer falls dead.

Fourth is *the impossible dream* (24%), which is divorced from reality, symbolic, and powerfully moving. Dreams of this type are like our ordinary hallucinatory nightmares; for the veteran, he may be dreaming only partly of Vietnam. Healing takes time and patience.

> He that lacks time to mourn, lacks time to mend. Eter-
> 　　nity
> mourns that, 'Tis an ill cure for life's worst ills, to have
> not time to feel them. Where sorrow's held intrusive

and
turned out, there wisdom will not enter, nor true
    power,
nor ought that dignifies humanity.[4]

Solzhenitsyn has asked: "Is it possible to transmit the experience of those who have suffered to those who have yet to suffer?
Can one part of humanity learn from the bitter experience of another? Is it possible to warn someone of danger?"[5]

At times my work with these men was stressful and painful,
and many times I asked myself why I had taken it on, or rather,
why it had taken me on. I felt a compelling interest: It was as if I
had started a journey from which I could not turn back. There were
times when I myself had war nightmares; then I knew that the ten-
sion and suffering of my patients were getting to me. I took off a
few days from working with the veterans. When all of the interviews were finished, I listened to the audiotapes as I reviewed the
typed transcriptions and my notes. I could understand the end of
Shakespeare's *King Lear*:

The weight of this sad time we must obey;
Speak what we feel, not what we ought to say.[6]

Listening attentively in a nonjudgmental way is the key to
helping the healing process: by accepting the dreamer and his
dreadful images and memories. However, caution should be the
watchword in dealing with war nightmares; no one should attempt
to interpret them unless he, the listener, has had experience working with dreams, or has someone experienced in this field to help.
But attentive nonjudgmental listening is therapeutic because it re-
tells another's story in a manner relatively free of conscious distortion.

The reception of the soldiers when they arrived in the United
States can be illustrated by the account of Mike—wounded, fright-

[4]H. Taylor, *Philip van Artevelde*, part I, act 1, sc. 5, line 38.
[5]Alexander Solzenitzen, "Wake Up! Wake Up!" *Readers Digest*, December,
1975, p. 69.
[6]William Shakespeare, *King Lear*, act 5, sc. 3, lines 323–324.

ened, feeling guilty for having survived when his buddies had been killed, yet happy to be home. He said to me:

> I arrived at the San Francisco airport and went to a bar. The people at the bar said, "Well, what are you doing here? You're crazy. Why don't you get the hell out of here?" It seemed to me that the media had depicted us as being crazy and when I left the service I considered myself normal. I just wanted to get out. I did my thing, and now leave me alone.

Tom, who prided himself on being a grunt (a foot soldier) who spent twenty-six months in Vietnam, survived the Tet Offensive at Hue, when it was captured by the Vietcong and the North Vietnamese. He told me about how it was when he landed in Washington, D.C. at the National Airport: "A lady came up to me and called me 'a murderer,' and hit me in the face with her purse. I said, 'Shit! This is what I came home to?' I went and got a drink. I didn't want to come home if this was how it was gonna be."

Cervando, a tough, ex-Marine with a drawer full of medals, said to me: "Look around you. There are still people who are ashamed to say, 'I'm a Vietnam veteran because I'm scared that people won't talk to me.' I've been insulted. 'Sir, were you one of them butchers over there? Did you enjoy killing babies and people?'"

I need not repeat the endless shameful ways in which many veterans were "welcomed" by being spit on and humiliated, stereotyped as losers, baby killers, dope fiends, and walking time bombs.

Phil told me his recurrent haunting nightmare: "I see this kid twelve or thirteen years old with his leg blown off, telling us in Vietnamese to go home and let the people do their own fighting. At the same time he was yelling to kill us. I turned away and someone killed him."

Eric, who lost his right foot in a grenade explosion, said to me: "When they used to ask me, 'Hey were you in Vietnam?' or 'What happened to your leg?' I'd say I had a car accident so I didn't have to bring it up. But all I was doing was lying to myself." Eric had the following dream several times a week:

> We are on a search and destroy mission and going through a "friendly" native village. A baby was crying in a hooch. No one was around anywhere. A buddy went into the hooch where the crying was. The

captain yelled: "Don't pick it up!" My buddy didn't hear the warning, and reached for the baby. The baby was booby-trapped with a grenade. It exploded. There were only parts of the soldier and nothing recognizable of the baby.

He reflected on the dream, which he recalled as being exactly like the real event. "I couldn't see shooting children, kids that don't have a chance in the world. I have two children of my own, but over there they used children against us. I couldn't understand why we had to kill children and why we were over there. There was nothing left to do over there, after you see dead kids. And that baby—I'll never get that baby out of my mind. Never."

> Unnatural deeds
> Do breed unnatural troubles.[7]

Mike, a paraplegic veteran, was shot in the back by "friendly fire" when one of his buddies fell and accidentally fired his M16 rifle, severing Mike's spinal cord. Now he had excruciating muscle cramps in his legs and was confined to a wheel chair. He said: "Vietnam had been a high for me. Here I was, seventeen years old, and that shit was better than any combat movie I ever saw. It was for real. Sometimes I would think it would have been nice to have stayed there."

On only a few occasions did he bemoan his terrible fate or ask the question: What if I had stayed? He dreamed that the Americans had turned on him as if he was the enemy. They tied him to a tree and threw axes at him. At other times he dreamed he was a POW being captured by the Americans. When he was flown back to Texas he weighed only eighty pounds and was sent to the hospital at Fort Sam Houston in San Antonio.

Mike recalled no dreams at all while in Vietnam. His recurrent nightmare was of the time when

> We stacked bodies. One was the guy we called "Coke bottle" because of his thick glasses. They blew the top of his head off. "Pick him up, man!" There were pieces of brain and shit on my boots. We took the bodies to the LZ and AK45s were cracking. "Pass the word. They got

---

[7]William Shakespeare, *Macbeth*, act 5, sc. 1, lines 79–80.

Coke Bottle." We dropped napalm. I dug in scared, crying my ass off. "Maybe he's not dead." There was artillery fire all night. I fell asleep and had a frightening dream of sounds like elephants coming at me. I woke up screaming. We moved out in the morning. They lifted Coke Bottle sitting up in a hoist to a chopper, red hair, blood and all.

After a few months, Mike's nightmares stopped and his deep depression lifted, but about the same time he began to bleed from the bowels and was admitted to Ward 13 at Fort Sam Houston. He thought it was fate because when he first came back from Vietnam he was admitted to Ward 13 on the thirteenth day of the month. "There was something about the ward from the first day I saw it," he said to me. "It seemed like it was going to be a part of me for the rest of my life." Though he was afraid of the depression, it did not come back.

The dreams I have about Vietnam now are all about day patrols and no action. I don't know why they changed. Maybe it's because I'm seeing you. In the past if I had one of these flashbacks I'd start trembling and sweating. It would worry the hell out of me. Now I can sit back and accept the fact that talking about Vietnam is not going to change anything. I don't think of Vietnam. . . . But how the hell can I live like this, Doc?

Mike was referring to the colostomy the surgeons had performed when they removed his cancer, which he was convinced had been caused by Agent Orange. The last time I visited him at the hospital the ward was crowded and Mike was semiconscious. I thought of his visit to me at Christmas nine months before when he had told me how he envied the Vietnamese' simple life and their beautiful country. "I never hated the Vietnamese," he said. Two of the Vietnam veterans in his group at the vet center had developed cancer. Mike wondered out loud to me, "What would I say if a doctor told me I had so many months to live? I'd probably go ape-shit." He didn't. He died rather peacefully.

I reflected: it was good that his nightmares and flashbacks and depression had been relieved. But at that time he began to have his symptoms of cancer. That was bewildering and disheartening. For a brief moment I wondered if he would have been better off with his depression, as if that had warded off the cancer rather than heralding it. I thought I did the best I could. Mike did the best he could. His healing nightmares had done their work. The relief of the depression and nightmares, I believe, helped his dying.

As in many other times and circumstances in my life as a doctor, I felt despair and helplessness in facing the death of someone who had bared his soul to me. Reviewing all the audiotapes of our meetings, I could find no clue to show that Mike's unconscious mind was reacting to the growing tumor or his coming death, not even in his dreams. Perhaps, as Jung noted, the unconscious does not take much notice of our death, but rather reacts to our attitudes toward dying. Still, I asked myself, why had all of this seemed to happen just as his spirits were lifted, and his life was more joyful? Was it possible he sought me out because the depression had been the alarming signal of impending peril? It is true that life never turns out quite as we expect it. When Mike was comatose and dying, I wanted very much to say something that he could hear, but I didn't know what to say, and the silence was closing in.

I have cited two Vietnam veterans whose nightmares helped their healing process, but naturally, for most of the veterans I saw, all I could do was to give them a sort of handle on the dreams and help them understand that their dreams were part of the healing process.

I was convinced that there was meaning, and I was trying to help them search for that meaning. I was reassured that life was not "a tale told by an idiot." There was meaning to be found in chaos and disorder, and meaning was the source of inner growth.

The survivors' most disturbing and most haunting nightmares were of the killing of their buddies—psychologically, the sacrifice of the brother. Next most disturbing were the killing of children and infants, the killing of women, and atrocities. The least distressful nightmares were the killing of enemy soldiers. These were the business of dreams of war.

It is important to be able to take the psychological step of recognizing an inner reality, an inner world, just as valid as the outer reality, though of a different order. This inner world also is the place of spirit and the collective unconscious in which we are one with all humanity, with human beings, at all times, and at all places.

Here is the archetypal world in which Jung formulated the concept of "the shadow," the dark side of the psyche, the rejected

Speakers Robert Bly (*left*) and Harry Wilmer.

Washington Post columnist Philip Geyelin gives his address.

Walt Rostow fields a question.

Historian George C. Herring.

The audience listens as historian George Herring makes his remarks.

Questions from the audience contributed to the proceedings. Here Texas lawyer Maury Maverick poses a question.

Small-group discussions allowed further exploration of the issues raised by the speakers.

Vietnam veteran John Contee makes a point in a small-group discussion.

and unwanted, suppressed and repressed unconscious that to Freud was the unconscious but to Jung was a deeper part of the unconscious—that which does not originate in the life of the individual but is inherent in the human psyche—the collective shadow that, ultimately, is absolute evil.[8]

Until Vietnam, Americans were content to see the shadow and evil only in their enemies. But with the Vietnam experience, the media—and the living-room video-war (reaching its best production in the PBS "Vietnam: A Television History") changed that. Suddenly technology not only let us see the close-up horror of war but also let us see it as it was happening. That has never happened before in the history of the world.

Until a few years ago we were content to let the veterans carry the odious burden of our collective shadow while most of us repressed what we knew, what we had seen. Now we in America are becoming a conscious part of the collective shadow of civilization. The archaic part of the psyche, the shadow, is the instinctual, the animal, part of the psyche. This is clearly seen in the mutual projection of evil between the Communists and the Americans. The shadow is the Mr. Hyde to our Dr. Jekyll—you remember Robert Louis Stevenson's story of Dr. Jekyll and Mr. Hyde, a story based on *his* personal nightmare. The story is about a philanthropic doctor who invented a powder by which he could transform himself into his own opposite. Many of the veterans I saw described themselves in the metaphor of "Dr. Jekyll and Mr. Hyde." Inevitably the consequences of unleashing powers of good and evil to go their separate ways was a fatal mistake. The integration of good and evil is the only way to heal the nightmare. That is what the transpersonal psyche is trying to do in dreams of Vietnam.

The archetypes of the collective unconscious not only manifest themselves as the shadow, but also as many other archetypes, both positive and negative. The shadow is a menace only so long as it remains unconscious and we fail to own our own darkness. Unless we become conscious of this shadow, we will know it only in our projections onto other people, other races, other nations, and other

---

[8]Carl G. Jung, "The Fight with the Shadow," in *Collected Works*, vol. 3, (Princeton: Princeton University Press, 1970), 218–26.

ideas. Being conscious of the shadow may lead to constructing positive changes in attitude.

For the American people, the Vietnam War revealed the American shadow in an almost inescapable way. The horrors and atrocities were not only committed by the enemy but also by us, the collective—as is true in all wars. But the American shadow had never been so conspicuous since the Civil War, when brother fought brother and a quarter of a million lives were lost, when a million men were wounded, when the slaves were freed. The shadow of war and division in the country was never again so clear until after Vietnam. No one who has not seen war can imagine exactly what war is like. I submit that the most readily available personal way to know what it is like is to experience the veteran's dream world. Through this experience it is possible to see war in a way that no traditional clinical psychiatric or psychological study could reveal. Statistical analyses give us only the impersonal facts; in them an individual is nothing but a unit. We know about the atrocities at My Lai and the shooting of children in cold blood. But do we know what was the real problem in the killing of babies and children? The real problem was that one had to kill them because they were, or were thought to be, armed or booby-trapped.

George, another veteran survivor of the battle at Hue, remembers all of the sights and sounds—the napalm, mortars, bombing, rockets, pounding, night after night. His nightmares began a year after he was home, and they have continued, not about Hue and its thousands of casualties, but about another time that he described to me from his dream in this way:

> We get into this village about six miles north of Da Nang, a bunch of little children are running towards us. The captain yells, "Fire!" When we fire, they explode. They are loaded with grenades. They were booby-trapped. They didn't disintegrate, they just blew to pieces. That's what's shattering my nerves.

I do not know how often this occurred statistically, but it occurred often enough that the men involved in it, those who heard about it from buddies, and those who became psychological casualties carried a heavy burden of guilt and a great sadness for these events.

Wilson, a marine sergeant who had been in combat in Korea and Vietnam, had this nightmare:

> There was a big flash and everybody is hurting and crying for the corpsman, "Medic! Medic!" Then everybody is kinda lying there hearing the helicopters come in. And an army lieutenant is walking across the knoll with no foot. It was blown off. I hear him getting on board the damn helicopter dragging the bone across the steel deck and—damn that hurts to look at it. He didn't even know what was happening. I wake up sweating and say, "Oh shit! That happened all over again." I get a real bad headache then. I just lay there. I feel like someone has put an axe between my ears, and I just feel like everything is coming apart at the seams. I lay there trying to relax, waiting for the sun to come up. I can't sleep.

It is not surprising that Wilson cannot bear the sound of chalk scratching on a blackboard.

Now a dream about identification with the dead, and grief and guilt. Mario, a tall, brooding, muscular ex-Marine, was sent home to escort the body of a buddy who had been his childhood friend. Mario said:

> I came back to stand in the funeral with two other Marines as honor guard. My buddy's wife came up to me and said, "Why did you let him die?" I just flipped out there. I took off out of the funeral home and for a long time I held that guilt within me. I wasn't sure if it was my fault or not. Maybe she just needed someone to blame it on. When I went back to Vietnam, I went back to be killed. I really didn't want to go back home at all. Now I have a nightmare about how it actually happened:
> My buddy gets hit. I am close enough to reach him, but I can't do anything. He is dying. The right side of his head is totally gone. It looks like hamburger, and the other side is a mess. I don't know what hit my buddy, but for some ungodly reason he is still alive. I hold him between my legs and he more or less bleeds to death.

That is the psychological, social, and physical reality of death. *That* is the bravery and selflessness and the story of the hero who became the antihero. *That* is what the conflagration of war does to individuals. *That* is the primitive basis of the pain which comes when people are slaughtered. And there are no words to articulate what happened. No one wants to hear anyway.

> To sleep—perchance to dream. Aye, there's the rub,
> For in that sleep of death what dreams may come,[9]

There was a recurrent theme in the fourth category of dreams, a theme that might be either possible or impossible, because it is not our reality. This is the kind of dream I am referring to:

> I am trying to warn people that another war is coming, and people are laughing at me. I am in Dallas and we are going in a chopper to secure a position. I am trying to warn people: "Hey! There's a war fixing to happen! You'd better take cover and get off the street!" But they were laughing and scoffing and they wouldn't listen to me. I was trying to reason with the people when the helicopters flew off and left me there. I woke up angry because I couldn't get the people to understand what was really happening.

This veteran said:

> The dream is probably related to when I first came back from Nam and tried to tell people and they wouldn't believe me. They refused to listen. Some laughed, and in the middle of it all I completely lost my ability to communicate with these people. It was like in the dream when Uncle Sam and his chopper fly off and leave me there. It's the last link I have. Without it I'm not a part of the unit anymore.

He reflected: "Maybe all these dreams that are circling in my mind are trying to give me the same message, that I feared all these last ten years taking responsibility for being a mortal being."

We need all the moral courage we have to come to terms with our errant shadow. We cannot do so like surgeons cutting it out and sewing up the wound. The shadow is not in our physical-material reality. We must give up some of our cherished ideals, not because they are wrong, but because the ideals and expectations were raised too high or based on illusion or sham.

Learning about the psychological effects of catastrophic trauma is of importance to each one of us, not only on behalf of soldiers who have died, but of those who have survived and want us to know what war is really like, so that we can be prepared, so that we can try to stop another war from happening, another Vietnam. If we

---

[9]William Shakespeare, *Hamlet*, act 2, sc. 1, lines 65–66.

face the responsibility of being mortal human beings, the healing process—in both our national and our individual nightmares—may change in the light. We will also do this so that our children and our grandchildren and the children to come after them will have a safe world and not endure a nuclear war—limited or unlimited. We owe this to ourselves and to our families and to each other.

This begins not with all of us, as a collective, but with each one of us individually, because the human mind is the greatest power on earth. If we are individually informed and can individually achieve some measure of peace we can hope for peace in the outer world.

Most of the Vietnam combat veterans have adjusted well to civilian life. Those whom I studied still suffer. They were unlucky enough to have been caught in a tragic situation. It is condescending to look upon these men as weak or as aberrations. It is our weakness not to be able to face that, given the same circumstances, had we been they, we would have suffered the same. Northrup Frye reflected that each one alone is "innocent in the sense of what happens to him, is far greater than anything he has done provokes, like the mountaineer whose shouts bring down an avalanche and he is guilty in the sense that he is living in a world where injustices are an inescapable part of existence."[10] That is the collective guilt we all share.

We can still learn about the psychological trauma of war from veterans of our last war. Time is running short. Other Vietnams are lurking.

I am seeking to understand the way in which the mind copes with violence and death in the hope that this awareness will contribute to understanding the enduring effect of war on the psyche of the individual soldier. My friend, the late Eric Hoffer, observed that "In the alchemy of men's souls, almost all the noble attributes, courage, honor, love, hope, faith, duty and loyalty—can be transmuted into ruthlessness. Compassion alone stands apart from the continuous traffic between good and evil proceeding within us.

[10]Northrup Frye, *Anatomy of Criticism* (Princeton: Princeton University Press, 1973), pp. 33–43.

Thus the survival of the species may depend on the ability to foster a boundless capacity for compassion."[11] It is far better to light the darkness than to turn our backs on it, and infinitely safer. Dreams of Vietnam can be thought of as the healing nightmare of the individual, symbolic of the healing national nightmare. Healing depends upon each of us hearing this new, frightening, and hopeful frontier of the human psyche. My study is an infinitesimal part of our task. We may diminish the fears and the horrors by facing them. When we do face them, we may then reveal our soldiers' bravery, begin to honor the men and women who suffer the psychological trauma of violence. Compassion for these survivors and for those who died helps us understand the meaning of healing, helps us understand what is holy, and what is whole. We are all a part of the Vietnam experience and its awesome heritage.

[11]Eric Hoffer, *Before the Sabbath* (New York: Harper and Row, 1979), p. 99.

LYNDA E. BOOSE

The Salado Symposium:
Afterword

IN the fall of 1982 the Vietnam War was once again very much on
the minds of Americans. After nearly a decade of silence, our nation's newspapers, magazines, and radio and television networks,
reminded us that the Vietnam War legacy lives on. There had been,
of course, some painful reminders along the way—the television
documentary *The 10,000 Day War*, the book *Fire in the Lake*, the
film *Apocalypse Now*, or, for that matter, memoirs of generals and
hearings before the House of Representatives Subcommittee on
Veterans Affairs—but the nation as a whole had manipulated its
collective mind to put the Vietnam experience behind it. The veterans of that war, however, told us that while the nation might want
to repress that history, it could not forget the actors—the soldiers
who carried out the policies, programs, and military operations of
the principal shapers of that history. If the government would not
take the lead in publicly recognizing their service, they would. On
November 11, 1982—Veterans Day—one-half million Americans
gathered in Washington, D.C., to dedicate the long-postponed
Vietnam Veterans Memorial. As the television cameras recorded
the events of that day, citizens across the country witnessed anew
the tragic legacy of the Vietnam War.

Two weeks prior to Veterans Day, 1982, a small group of Americans gathered in an unlikely place—Salado, Texas, forty-five miles
to the north of Austin—to "understand" Vietnam. These 159 Americans spent the better part of three days and two nights listening to
formal addresses, participating in small-group discussions, viewing
a new documentary film of the war, revealing to each other the
pain, sorrows, and, yes, accomplishments too, of the Vietnam ex-

perience. For these Americans, the war and its aftermath had not been repressed. But who were they, and why did they go to Salado?

They came from the cities of Texas—Houston, Dallas, San Antonio, El Paso—and from smaller towns as well—Belton, Temple, Marlin, Huntsville; 105 men and 54 women. At the conclusion of the symposium, 64 of them took the time to complete a detailed evaluation of the conference, and from their responses, we get some clues as to why these people chose to give up an October weekend to learn more about Vietnam.

Most of those attending were between forty-four and fifty-three years old; they would have been between twenty-five and thirty-six when the Tonkin Gulf resolution was passed by Congress in 1964, and between thirty-three and forty-four when U.S. military troops were officially hurriedly withdrawn from Vietnam in 1973. They were predominantly white Americans (87%), but some Mexican Americans and blacks were also present. They were people of many professions and occupations: teachers, counselors, doctors, laborers, army officers, lawyers, business people, homemakers, and journalists. Nearly 20 percent of those who completed the questionnaire were veterans of the Vietnam era, with half of those veterans having served in combat. Approximately 15 percent indicated that their most direct connection with the war was being a close relative of a soldier who served; approximately 25 percent identified themselves as war protesters; and 45 percent indicated that they had no direct personal involvement in Vietnam.

Views on the war differed extensively. The largest percentage of those responding—over 30 percent—said that their initial opinion that the war was a moral and human waste had not changed over the years. But 25 percent indicated a dramatic change in attitude, from early idealistic support of U.S. goals to ultimately feeling that the United States should not have been in Vietnam and that America had been betrayed by its policymakers. Others originally supported the war and continue to feel that it was right; others were opposed to the war at first but in retrospect think that our presence in Vietnam was justified. In short, the wide range of attitudes that constituted American reaction to the war in the 1960s was in evidence among those attending the Vietnam symposium. But why did they come to Salado? Over 95 percent of those completing the questionnaire expressed a strong belief that the Vietnam experience required additional public discussion and thought that such anslysis, gained through conferences and other programs, could lead to a stronger retrospective public reaction against the war and a consequent determination to "never let such a debacle as the Vietnam War occur again," as one person put it. Others felt the value of the symposium lay in its ability to disseminate information and to inform the public about a war it had progressively tuned out of its consciousness. Some, at the end of the symposium, could point to tangible benefits, such as Robert Bly's pledge to initiate a "writers in support of Vietnam veterans" group, or Lawrence Kolb's pledge to carry ideas back to the Veterans Administration, or Douglas Kinnard's public statement that he now saw himself as a veteran of the war and would begin to work with veterans groups in his home state. Most, however, pointed to more subtle and less tangible benefits that they felt came through the public-discussion program. Many recalled the extreme polarization of Americans during the war and were grateful for the chance to meet their former enemy on neutral ground, to express their feelings and even their doubts, and to recognize that certain shared values still exist even among those with differing viewpoints. In the words of one combat veteran: "Feelings and emotions are an important part of war that books don't always communicate very well; real people do better in situations such as conferences." Similar answers tell us that many who came to Salado desired not only to understand more deeply one another's experiences, but to break down the safety of distance, to be close to those who may have held a radically differing position, to see one another as Americans.

Above all, the questionnaires indicate that those who attended the Salado Symposium—regardless of specific positions held on the war—shared a certain kind of public guilt over the Vietnam experience and sought absolution. Such guilt was once confined almost entirely to the veteran himself, but had somehow been recycled, finding a place in the psyche of those who had not fought. After reading each questionnaire, I concluded that there were present in Salado many people who had remained morally untarnished by having stayed at a distance from the Vietnam War but who, by 1982, needed to work through the history and nature of the war and through their sense of guilt in the presence of veterans. The pressing issue had become not the war, which most still strongly opposed, but a need to open and cleanse some closed-off wound in the psyche that still festered with the rancor of the past. As one person put it, "In this public discussion, the presence of these veterans made the nightmare more real, and the healing more possible." In the cleansing process, the wounded veterans had paradoxically become the conference physicians.

The decision of these Americans to attend a Vietnam symposium provoked considerable anxiety. There were those who feared that the program somehow or another would be a distortion of reality or, worse, a whitewash of the past presidential administration. Others felt that the discussion might get too emotional and confrontational, and some indicated that they feared that the symposium would provoke old memories, would unleash feelings of anger and resentment. Interestingly, the war protesters, compared with veterans and those not personally involved in the war, appear to have had the highest anxiety level. In thinking about the symposium, one such protester stated: "It recalled the war and its divisions vividly and brought up personal issues that remain difficult for me now." Another said: "It [the symposium] would be a reentry into the issue which had been so important in my life for seven years. I was anxious about my reaction to Walt Rostow, whom I had felt was such a monstrous figure during the war that I didn't know if I could be in the same room with him." He was relieved "not to feel hatred toward him, nor have anything to fear in my reaction to him."

And how did these people—these Americans who desired to remember rather than to forget the past—react to the symposium itself? By going back to the discussions that took place during the symposium, and by reviewing the completed questionnaires, a preliminary assessment is possible. First, a brief summary of some of the dialogue.

Interesting discussion occurred during the time reserved for "questions and answers" following each of the major presentations. A Vietnam veteran, now working as a counselor, challenged George Herring on the possible economic roots of the war, something not covered by Herring in his paper. Herring acknowledged "that there were some businesses that did profit in some way, out of war construction and the like," but asserted that, by and large, American companies had little invested in Southeast Asia, and thus the war could not be seen as a means of protecting American investments overseas. Another veteran asked Herring whether "it would have been possible in 1954 and the year following for us to encourage the development of a regime which would have belonged more to the people of South Vietnam than either of the possibilities that survived in the sixties." Answered Herring: "Maybe, but could we do it as an outside nation who had been identified with the French, who knew virtually nothing about the people and culture of Vietnam?"

Questions and comments stimulated by Douglas Kinnard's paper centered more on policymaking. An active army general, stationed in Texas, said: "If our country finds that our interest requires us to go to war—and I pray to God, first of all, that that never happens again—but if it does, that there be a national consensus with very clear strategic national objectives which must be the backdrop against which military objectives are selected. In Vietnam they were not clear at all."

A former staff member of the Johnson administration asked Kinnard whether an objective could have been given to General Westmoreland that would have accomplished a military victory. Kinnard responded: "I don't think it was possible, given the constraints that we fought under, in terms of a military victory as you mean it."

Walt Rostow responded to Kinnard's address: "If we had seen it through, South Vietnam would have moved the way South Korea has. In fact, during the war, it was much more advanced than South Korea was during the Korean War. . . . You left out elements that I would regard, going back to Dr. Wilmer's words, as true horror, a dark side of America, which was the action in 1975 of the Congress in cutting the aid to the South Vietnamese in half. . . . In the words of a victorious general, published in the *New York Times*, it was those cuts in aid . . . which broke the morale of the South Vietnamese."

Walt Rostow's paper elicited questions about his underlying assumptions. One person remarked: "I can see a Soviet professor up on the lectern lecturing and pointing out the same strategic places, saying that is the threat of the American interest. . . . Well, this is a vast geopolitical football game." Rostow responded: "We are in a historical situation in which out of historical circumstances, we have developed certain interests, for example, having no hostile power control of the Atlantic or the Pacific. . . . Our national interests are not written out in the Constitution, but they are the natural and abiding interests of an island. . . . We are the natural friends of those who, for their own reason, do not wish in their regions to be dominated by a potentially hostile power. . . . I don't believe the Soviets are born with any more original sin than we are . . . but they are in the real-estate business. They are of a deep conviction that it is their historical duty, as both Russians and as Communists, to expand their powers as far as they can."

This response led Philip Geyelin to remark: "I don't see this picture of an expansionist Soviet Union in the real-estate business. Where is the real-estate business, other than Afghanistan, which they have moved into? I just don't understand how the Soviet Union shapes up as a country that is going to take the risk of a nuclear war to shut off—what? Japanese tankers on their way to the Persian Gulf? . . . I just have the sense from the way you picture this that we were in mortal peril."

Robert Bly's presentation elicited response at a deeper, more emotional level. A woman in the audience countered sharply: "I am sorry I can't get too worried about the disappearance of male values. I don't think it is radical to suggest that that is how we got into the nightmare of Vietnam and that is the reason we didn't get out when we should have. . . . Your traditional male values are alive and well. Fifteen miles to the north in Temple, Texas, ten-year-old boys are told to beat the hell out of each other every Saturday morning in football."

An army general responded: "I think poets are much more important to society than generals, just to make sure that we are straight on that. . . . I'm not sure whether you are extraordinarily wise or terribly naive, and I am not even sure which one I hope that it is. For whatever it is worth, there are some other perspectives. There were, believe it or not, in addition to some horrible things and some very poor leadership, there were some compassionate, understanding, and courageous people who were trying to lead American soldiers in a very tough situation. I agree that Abraham Lincoln was a rare leader, but of course, we also recognize that in one of his battles there were more Americans killed than in the entire Vietnam War."

Walt Rostow also responded to Bly. "It would be very wrong if we did not have on this program someone like Mr. Bly to capture the raw revolt, the ugliness of this war as it was deeply felt by many, including above all, people like President Johnson and Secretary Rusk. . . . I want to try to make clear to you the human depth of the problem of dealing with nuclear weapons in the early 1960s. The responsibility lay on one man, the president of the United States. No one knows what odds were on the possibility of a nuclear engagement over the confrontation in Berlin or the Cuban missile crisis . . . but any risk of a nuclear war to a president of the United States represented more than any human being should have to bear. One can protest and cry out from the heart as you did, Mr. Bly, and it would be wrong if you didn't, but we live in a world with nuclear weapons and the first responsibility felt by President Kennedy and President Johnson was to protect the interest of this society in a world which is not a global government, but a world of sovereign states in ways which minimize the risk that nuclear weapons would have to be used. . . . In the choices that they faced . . . the minimization of any risk of nuclear war was paramount."

A teacher from a nearby university asked Philip Geyelin: "How might we think about approaching consensus in ways that we have not? How do we achieve consensus on foreign policy?" Geyelin answered: "There are all kinds of techniques . . . background press conferences, some effort to deal with the press, even if you can't say something publicly, at least try to explain things privately. . . . The problem with Vietnam was that it dawned on us after awhile that even what we were being told privately wasn't true. . . . If you have to strike a balance between cutting the American public in or not. . . . I say you better cut the American public in because sooner or later it will catch up."

In response to a question from the audience about whether or not our national interests were at stake in Vietnam, Geyelin responded: "Although horrible things happened after we pulled out and [although] the South Vietnamese lost the war, I still don't quite accept Professor Rostow's dark view of what's going to happen to the rest of Southeast Asia. I don't think the dominoes did all fall."

Questions addressed to Harry Wilmer concentrated on issues related to the mental and physical health of veterans and on the healing process. There were numerous questions on Wilmer's methods of treatment, on the rate of success through psychiatric care, and on particular issues such as suicide and drug abuse. The veterans, in particular, were interested in the personal healing process. Said one: "Did you find in any of the individuals who seemed to be progressing that the dreams changed from one class or kind to another?" Answered Wilmer: "Oh yes, that is when I thought something was happening. When something began to change, when you began to talk to them and all of a sudden it wasn't the same dream they had been having for years, then I thought there was a chance. And that is when things began to heal."

Another person asked: "One of the things that comes through very strongly in your address has to do with the incredible cruelty of a relentless and ruthless enemy. I wonder if we have ever as a nation been exposed, face to face, with cruelty like that of attaching, for example, grenades to babies, and whether that has something to do too with the trauma that our men suffered there?" Wilmer answered: "At first I thought that this was the worst war, but as I listened to the soldiers, as I read, as I looked at films, as I talked to men who had been in other wars, I came to the conclusion that it wasn't any more horrible than any other war. We were closer to the horror, we heard more about it, and we saw it, but I don't think it exceeded other wars."

Someone asked whether Wilmer had received encouragement from others for his work with veterans. Wilmer answered that "with the exception of my students, I got no support at all. In fact, quite the opposite." And, finally, a woman responded to the presentation: "You forgot to mention that there were also female vets who were in Vietnam and who are also trying to come out of the closet and who are having nightmares."

Those who completed the questionnaire at the conclusion of the symposium offered their thoughts on the major presentations.

Robert Bly was both praised and damned for the emotional

style of and the demands inherent in his presentation. In the words of some, "he dared to confront us"; "he spoke to, not about the suffering"; he "brought home the real ugliness of the war like no one else did"; "he reminded us that America has yet to grieve for its errors." Others, however, felt anger over his poems, arguing that he "put on a performance," was "out of touch with reality," and that his "logic was wrong and inaccurate."

Philip Geyelin was most appreciated for what was perceived as his sympathetic approach to differing perspectives on the war. He was valued for presenting "a good overview of the way the war impacted on society" and "for saying we did the right thing in the wrong war." Others, however, faulted Geyelin for "not taking the opportunity to suggest ways to harness the best side of the Vietnam syndrome, especially in regard to the problem of the consent of the governed."

Douglas Kinnard was repeatedly cited for embodying compassion. Apparently, the idea of a military general who had thought deeply about the military effort and who radiated compassion surprised many people; in the words of one: "He broke through my stereotype." He was highly valued by some because "after he had spoken, he demonstrated that the conference had touched him and made him aware of the veteran's problem. He showed that even an authority on the subject was willing to learn." He showed "a candid, military understanding that came from a military man who was willing to expose rather than try to defend the U.S. actions in Vietnam, both the political and military ones." A veteran stated that "he helped me understand some of the strategy, events, and modes of operation that I'd been a part of." In the words of another, "He was a wise soldier."

Walt Rostow's historical analysis generated little warm response but he was valued by most of the participants, perhaps ironically, because, in the words of one: "He took me inside the bureaucratic mind and showed me how far morality was divorced from the politics of the war," and because he "so clearly represented unchanged all the attitudes, thinking, and absence of feeling of the government during the war. . . . He was a mirror of the calm, self-assured, seeming certainty of the executive branch in those years." Others felt that "the blanketing, the cover-up, is still there," with an obsessive determination to defend Johnson's policies. Yet nearly everyone was glad that the program included Rostow. Said one: "I'm glad that Walt Rostow was brave enough to come."

Harry Wilmer was valued for the compassionate work he had done with the Vietnam veterans and for his leadership in organizing the symposium. Respondents specifically admired him "for bravely facing the uncomfortable feelings, the emotions, and the denied psyche," and "for forcing the veterans (and all of us) to confront rather than avoid the nightmares."

The symposium ended with a two-hour-long general discussion—a session that at times became intense. It began with summary comments by the major speakers, some ideas on "where to go from here." Each speaker had something useful to say, but Kinnard's statement moved many of the audience: "I must say that while I have played [at the symposium] the role of a college professor . . . this is the first real awareness I have had, the first sensitivity I have really had, to the veterans' problems in a personal way. I began to grasp this sometime yesterday and it dawned on me this morning that I was one of those veterans myself. I had not thought in those terms before. . . . I would like to say thank you for giving me a sensitiveness and awareness and I intend to pursue it on a personal basis, not as a college professor but as a veteran."

The rest of the program belonged to the veterans. Some eloquent, personal speeches ensued. Said one: "I was wounded in Vietnam. I was invited to this symposium. . . . I have had my memory refreshed as to the political aspects of Vietnam, but my primary concern is how am I going to go on and continue to live my life? What is being done for the people that served? There was nothing mentioned of Agent Orange. Is that going to affect me or my children? Veterans of World War II, of Korea, and of Vietnam all received entitlements, but we have yet to receive the sanction that those veterans received. I would not feel comfortable dressing up in my Special Forces uniform and marching in a Fourth of July parade because I did not receive that sanction. I have a lot of nightmares in the past. I have talked with Mr. Bly—he touched me very deeply. I did not sleep last night. I had a nightmare. The nightmare was the reality of the present. I have been sitting back. I got out of the service in 1973 and I have been sitting back without speaking out, without talking, without giving people my feelings. I am going to make myself heard. . . . But my primary question to you as a panel and to all of us is: What is going to be done now to give me and my brothers the sanction that is due them?"

Another veteran engaged in a verbal confrontation with Rostow. "I am a Vietnam vet, twice wounded. I served with the 101st Airborne Division. Right now I am feeling a lot of emotion, something that I have not seen displayed by Walt Rostow. And my question to you is, What are you going to do personally to help the veterans? You were advisory to the Johnson administration. Why was the use of defoliants and Agent Orange condoned and sprayed on our troops. What is the long-term effect?"

Walt Rostow answered: "Everyone has got to do what he thinks he can do and what is right as he sees it. I am a teacher. I am a historian. I am also a human being. What I felt that I could best do, I have done, which is to do the best, most honest historical analysis of the whole period from 1957 to 1972, including the analysis of why the decisions were made as they were by the United States government in that period. . . . Regarding Agent Orange, the decision on the use of the herbicides was made by the president on the recommendation of the military. The view at the time was that these were to be dropped in areas that were distant . . . because the deep cover gave protection to the Vietcong and the North Vietnamese. The analysis of the time, so far as I know . . . was that it would not do permanent damage to the environment or to human beings. . . . I don't know the answer, it may have been more damaging to human beings than was thought by the people at the time . . . but it was a device to deal with an enemy that was exploiting deep cover in distant places. . . . Every man has got to do what he thinks he can do best, and do it to his limit, and I have done that. If there is more that I can do, I will."

A veteran questioned a commanding general of an army base in Texas: "Sir, you told me you spent time in Vietnam working with the ARVN. Were you out there actually in combat, or was it just you and you know, a whole battalion behind you and circling around you, sir? And while I have the mike, I would like to make a suggestion. The next time [someone] puts something like this together, I would appreciate hearing from some of the ground troops, some who were down there swatting the mosquitos, who were down there saying, 'where in the hell is the ammo?'"

The general responded: "About half of my first tour I spent walking through the jungles with the Vietnamese Fortieth Infantry Regiment. Sometimes I had the patrol of the half-dozen folks and sometimes I had a whole regiment sneaking through the jungle one by one getting ambushed two or three times a day. I didn't see the war as a private soldier and I never told anybody I did, but I saw a lot of it, and I was with the Vietnamese about as much as any American was. So I have had folks killed next to me and I saw more bodies than most anybody in this room. I don't know all about the war either, and I tell you there were some damn brave Vietnamese, some of whom personally saved me. I agree that in a symposium like this it would be a good idea to get the input from a whole variety of people. . . . I have a lingering concern, and I hope a great interest in the soldiers who work for me now and who worked for me in Vietnam."

The soldier responded: "Thank you. Would it be possible . . . since you are a commanding general of the base where I once served . . . to talk to some of your officers. . . . I would like to address them on some of the things that I have been through. . . . I was there at the base once teaching hand-to-hand combat and map reading. I would like to be able to go back as a veteran to tell them about some of the problems that I am having now. Thank you, sir."

And the general: "We would be glad to have you any time. You can either talk about map reading, hand-to-hand combat, or your and my adjustment to post-Vietnam and we would be glad to welcome you any time."

Another veteran raised a perceptive question: "What should we be trying to do for the shattered countries, Vietnam and Cambodia? Shattered not just by the Vietnamese takeover but as the aftermath of thirty years of war which, after all, was mostly our idea. What should we be doing about the Indochinese refugees? This I am beginning for the first time to ask as a veteran. Perhaps veterans in particular have something to offer here."

Another veteran reminded the audience not to forget "those of whom we are most deeply ashamed and who are not here . . . those who ran away [from their military assignments]." And, finally, an audience member reminded the group that a woman was not included as a central speaker of the symposium. "Do we have to pound on the door and stomp our feet and come on strong to get in the door, or, are you going to include us? There are women who are living with the men who are having the nightmares. They are sleeping in the same bed. They are watching their family lives go down the drain with men who are on alcohol and drugs."

The questionnaires completed by the symposium participants included personal responses on issues related to Vietnam and to the symposium. The complexity of the issues to both those that led the United States into Vietnam and those the war left in its wake—is nowhere more apparent than in these responses. When participants were asked to focus on what, to each of them, was the most pressing issue to have come out of that aggregate of problems, perspectives, and emotions known as "Vietnam," their reactions covered a wide spectrum on two specific questions: (1) what future generations should be taught to "understand" about the Vietnam War and American participation in it and (2) what questions, ideas, views, or lessons were deemed the most important ones to come out of the Vietnam War era.

When focusing on these questions, some participants turned to the relationship of America with underdeveloped nations and defined either the source of the problem that led to Vietnam or the resolution of the problem as lying with American foreign policy and national attitudes of cultural chauvinism. The larger portion of respondents focused inward and located the problem or resolution with Americans' understanding of either the philosophical tenets of democracy or the practical application of citizen participation in the machinery of government. For some, the searing issue still to be addressed was the war itself, but the questions or lessons to be extrapolated from it differed widely. Some respondents generalized from the particular to the universal and felt the lesson to be learned from Vietnam was that war as an instrument of policy is without justification; others cautioned against making just this kind of association and using it to justify retreat into unconditional pacifism and global isolationism. Others emphasized the proclivity of history to repeat itself and felt the pattern of incremental government commitment to South Vietnam should, by analogy, spur us to force an immediate halt to the current escalation of U.S. military aid to El Salvador. And still others concentrated on trying to isolate what the problem had been in this particular war that made America, the superpower, end up in withdrawal and defeat—whether it could have been the lack of a coherently translatable military objective, the effects of the media on public support and military morale, or the limits and counterproductivity of the application of the most sophisticated weapons technology ever used in warfare.

Some respondents wanted the nation to focus not on why the war had happened or why the United States had failed but on how we can now treat the damage that the war psychologically wreaked upon the surviving veterans of that conflict. Others saw the preeminent lesson of Vietnam in the way the war exposed dangerous fissures in the bedrock of American society.

In terms of specific concepts and reactions, the participants' responses can be grouped around eleven areas.

1. In regard to U.S. foreign policy, some of the participants emphasized that the Vietnam War exposed a culpable enthocentricity and ignorance of and disregard for another society's history and cultural traditions. For instance, said one: "We must study cultures, governments, and problems of other countries and learn to work with them rather than dominate them." Said another: "Why do we try to force our way of life on peoples who don't seem to want it?" On a related matter, some of the participants focused on the gap between foreign-policy needs as recognized by presidential administrations, and needs recognized by the public, while others emphasized that the Vietnam War flowed from certain foreign-policy assumptions that hindsight may have shown to be false.

2. Some felt that the Vietnamese experience inevitably led to important considerations about democratic government. To one man, Vietnam had taught us about "the fragility of American democracy, the foibles and opportunities of democracy in crisis—the failure of government to educate the public and to level with the public in language that speaks clearly rather than muffles the truth,

and the failure of the public to insist on these things from the government." To another, the war made it clear that "the United States government is now autonomous from the people. The secret keepers, the policymakers in Washington, feel their understanding of all things is superior to that of the people they lead." Additional responses pointed to the need to reconnect democracy with its ideal of human rights, with its premise of openness, with the affirmation of the right to dissent, and with the necessity for a free press.

3. Various participants emphasized the internal need for Americans to become better informed about the concrete operation of their government, especially in regard to the question of legitimacy of fighting an undeclared war. Participants cited the need for more public information, for consensus as a precondition to U.S. involvement in any war, for the obligation to question and call our leaders to account, and for generally increased citizen involvement. Underlying these suggestions one finds the belief that had the citizenry been more informed and more determined to effect the course of their country, the Vietnam tragedy might have been avoided.

4. For some, the Vietnamese experience, and what they learned at the symposium, led to pacifism. "Is war ever necessary?" asked one. "There should be an *external* questioning of the idea that war is an inevitable solution to conflict." Another said: "War is never a solution—dialogue, economic sharing, and nonviolent resistance must be given a chance." And still another: "War is a terrible thing; therefore, we must never get ourselves into an undeclared war."

5. A good many of the participants focused on issues related to democracy and military action, especially in regard to fighting a limited war in a technological age. For these persons, the frustration of the Vietnam War exposed new truths about the intangible conditions necessary for success, truths that had lain unrecognized beneath the victorious gloss of American history. These recognitions included the need for the government to have a clearly articulated objective to give to both the commanders and soldiers on the war front and the public on the home front; the need for public support of the war effort and the men in it; the need for understanding of the problem that military constraints pose to combat units charged with the immediate task of defeating an enemy; and

the need for understanding the limits that the Vietnam War forced Americans to confront. These limits included the recognition "that the United States is not omnipotent nor omniscient," "recognition of the practical limits of American technological power," and recognition that "no matter how great a nation is, it can lose when pitted against the will of a people." One combat veteran summarized what he wanted future generations to understand: "That events can easily gain unwanted momentum in unpredicted directions; that limited war in a free society may not be possible; and that national will is a powerful force in determining any outcome."

6. Some concentrated their remarks—particularly nonveterans—on the psychological predicament of the veterans, both during and after the war. These comments focused on wanting current and future generations to understand the experiences and feelings of the men who fought in Vietnam; to appreciate the effect that the lack of moral support and the the lack of homecoming rituals had on this group of veterans; "to understand the frustration and bitterness felt by the Vietnam veterans . . . to understand the traumas experienced but also to understand that not all Vietnam veterans are drugged, crazy, psychotic, or babykillers." There is a recognition that healing for oneself ultimately depends upon healing the pain of the veterans: "To understand the veterans' position, to have compassion for them and be willing to try to contribute to their healing—and thus to my own."

7. Some of the participants who answered the questionnaire expressed a good deal of anger, stating that the Vietnam War was an inexcusable disaster that came about largely through the stubborn arrogance of government leaders who refused, out of misplaced pride, to withdraw from the calamity even after it was recognized as being one. "We made a bad war and then threw good blood after bad," said one. "It was a mistake," said another, "a tragedy. . . . The effects on the Vietnamese will never be known; the effects on the American veterans and the economy are still continuing." And another argued that the lesson of Vietnam is "awareness of psychophysical-spiritual damage done by wars which are motivated by lies and greed." And this foreboding comment: "Despite a change in the people who run the government, the 'mindset' of too many of our current national leaders has changed little since the

prewar days. It seems they have gained little insight from the events of the last twenty years from which to build new assumptions for the years to come."

8. The Vietnam War led some of the participants to reassess their attitudes toward government, with negative results. In the words of one, "Vietnam was the bursting of a boil long festering—a perfect example of the fruits of war and duplicity—the near demise of all the hope and ideals America has stood for. . . . What is now left of the image of America? Can it be restored?" One man, in his fifties, the father of two draft-age sons during the war, one of whom was a war protestor, describes his attitude toward U.S. involvement as one of initial support based on unquestioned acceptance of his government's decisions. In time, his attitude toward the war reversed, and he was left with a distrust of his own government: "My government made numerous statements which, as time passed, we discovered were lies, untruths, falsehoods. Now this distrust has spread to many areas of government activity." But, he adds, "perhaps this is a healthy situation. After all, our entire political structure was first organized on the basis of distrust of the power of governments. Perhaps we have all become complacent and have put too much trust and responsibility in government. Viligence is the price of liberty and we need to vigilently watch even well-meaning governments."

9. Some, however, while still acknowledging that the American intrusion into Vietnam was an error, nevertheless felt that the intentions of the United States were honorable and that that point should not be forgotten. "We came to discover," said one, "that despite largely generous motives, how wrong it was to be there." "There were some policies that were poor," said another, "but well intentioned." "A government can make a mistake," said another, "just as humans do." And finally, one woman in her sixties asks that future generations be willing "to understand enough to know that every generation does the best it can with its 'givens' and to be able to forgive us."

10. Some of the symposium participants felt that the Vietnam War highlighted gaps between various groups within American society, the young and old, the powerful and the powerless, the veterans of Vietnam and the veterans of other wars, men and women.

Some spoke about the difference between "national interest and the interest of the citizens," between the bureaucrats and the people, and between an autonomous U.S. government and the people. Finally, one woman, a military wife during the war, states that the most important thing that future generations could learn about Vietnam was "that it nearly destroyed all types of relationships in our country."

11. Finally, following the thought of Harry Wilmer, some of the participants who responded to the questionnaire focused on the war as the dark side of the self, and emphasized the need to accept that reality. Particularly, these people noted that Vietnam should be seen as the expression of an archetypal myth of the loss of innocence that compels the child to grow from happy naivete to responsible maturity. "Vietnam," said one, "finally shattered our myths of goodness and invincibility. . . . It was the event that ended our adolescence. Being who and what we were, we could have done no other than what we did there. We've had to learn to accept our own darker side that had been hidden in patriotic motives." One combat veteran states: "I feel that because I walked with the dark side of myself, I grew. I want the public now to explore their [our] dark side in such a fashion as to grow also." A former war protestor urges that "It is desperately important that some consciousness of the devastation this war wreaked on our souls and on our society be transmitted to future generations—and that we also transmit to them an owning up of our darkness and common humanity with other nations and peoples." And another respondent draws—for future generations—a vividly verbal picture of that dark shadow: "Man has a horrendous capacity for destruction and impersonality. In Vietnam all of us could look into that face and heart of darkness ourselves. And shudder."

In the responses of the veterans, one detects a thinly veiled, sometimes markedly defensive plea-request-demand for the American public to shoulder and share the burden that soldiers who fought in the first war that the United States ever lost now feel condemned to bear by themselves. The responses are significant not only because they differ so markedly from the others, but because they represent the voices of those who experienced Vietnam most directly.

In response to a question about what they wanted future generations to understand about U.S. participation in the Vietnam War, two veterans provided answers that are marked by a distinct confusion in the choice of pronouns, a confusion that strongly suggests ambiguity in the writers' identity and relationship to society. Said one: "Those of us who participated did so with honor, dignity, and to the best of their ability with the understanding and information available to them (i.e., us)." Said another: "That the American government and people lost this war, not the men who had to fight it. They should first make intelligent decisions whether to fight or not. Then if you do, support your troops, make a total commitment."

In the first quotation, the veteran begins by identifying himself in terms of "those of *us* who participated." But by midsentence he has dissocciated himself from his military participation and talks of the combat troops in terms of *their* ability and *them*. Then, after he finishes, he seems suddenly to remember the point of his sentence—to assert the integrity of his group—and consequently identifies *them* parenthetically as *us*.

In the second quotation, the respondent first lumps together the American government and people, to whom he attributes the loss of the war, and then polarizes these forces against the "men who had to fight it," a construction that betrays resentment, defensiveness, and a sense of injustice. His choice of pronouns then unconsciously displays the perception of another schism: In his second sentence he defines the decision-makers by the abstract *they*; in the third, he shifts references to characterize those who failed to support the troops by the more personal term, the collective and—in this context—the accusatory reference, *you*.

Other comments by the participating veterans are also telling: "Society should not identify the warrior with the bad war." "Without the nation's support, any war will be a lost cause from the onset." "[I want them] to learn the true reason for involvement and just why we fought the war the way we did." "Lessons: Without national will to win, the physical power of any military force may not prevail. A war can be won on the battlefield and lost in the living room." "I would like them to remember that we served our country with honor."

Taken as a whole, the completed questionnaires display an un-recognized ambivalence and an unshakeable optimism. On many a single form, despair competes with hope, distrust with loyalty, con-demnation with exculpation. The same questionnaire, for instance, that angrily speaks in one section of the government's inexcusable, immoral, and intransigent refusal to listen or learn subsequently betrays a competing wish to believe in the basic morality of that same government and excuses those actions by recharacterizing them as "well-intentioned mistakes."

One cannot, of course, make any accurate generalizations about how "Americans" feel about the Vietnam era from the basis of sixty-four questionnaires that describe in retrospect the attitudes of a doubly self-selected group of people in one section of the country who first chose to attend this symposium and then chose to submit their questionnaires for evaluation. Clearly, the study was not drawn from a random sample. But it has a quite different merit. Possibly, the contradictions and hopes reflected in these question-naire responses tell us just why the participants came, some nine years after the war presumably had ended, to spend a weekend in central Texas still trying to "understand" Vietnam. And just possibly the responses and the symposium from which they emerged em-blematically narrate something else: for as these 159 Americans grouped together in Salado, Texas, on the last weekend in October, 1982, one-half million others simultaneously began collecting in Washington, D.C., to dedicate the long-postponed Vietnam Veter-ans Memorial. Perhaps the responses from Salado indirectly nar-rate the story of why America could not honor its Vietnam dead for nearly a decade after the war, but why—on Veterans Day, 1982— it was finally able to do so. They tell us why this symposium on "Understanding Vietnam" was at once a conference and yet also something else—an undeclared requiem for an undeclared war.

Selected Bibliography

Books

Amter, Joseph A. *Vietnam Verdict: A Citizen's History.* New York: Continuum, 1982.

Baral, Jaya Krishna. *The Pentagon and the Making of U.S. Foreign Policy: A Case Study of Vietnam, 1960–1968.* Atlantic Highlands, N.J.: Humanities, 1978.

Baskier, Lawrence M., and William A. Strauss. *Chance and Circumstance: The Draft, The War, and the Vietnam Generation.* New York: Alfred A. Knopf, 1978.

Berman, Larry. *Planning a Tragedy: The Americanization of the War in Vietnam.* New York: Norton, 1982.

Blaufart, Douglas F. *The Counterinsurgency Era: U.S. Doctrines and Performance, 1950 to the Present.* New York: Free Press, 1977.

Blum, Robert M. *Drawing the Line: The Origin of the American Containment Policy in East Asia.* New York: Norton, 1982.

Bonds, Ray, ed. *The Vietnam War.* New York: Crown, 1979.

Braestrup, Peter. *Big Story: How the American Press and Television Reported and Interpreted the Crisis of Tet 1968 in Vietnam and Washington.* Garden City, N.J.: Anchor Press, Doubleday, 1978.

Bryan, C. D. B. *Friendly Fire.* New York: Putnam's, 1976.

Buttinger, Joseph. *Vietnam: The Unforgettable Tragedy.* New York: Horizon, 1977.

Capps, Walter H. *The Unfinished War: Vietnam and the American Conscience.* Boston: Beacon, 1982.

Caputo, Philip. *A Rumor of War.* New York: Holt, Rinehart, and Winston, 1977.

Carlton, Michael, and Anthony Moncrieff. *Many Reasons Why: The American Involvement in Vietnam.* New York: Hill and Wang, 1978.

Chandler, Robert W. *War of Ideas: The U.S. Propaganda Campaign in Vietnam.* Boulder, Colo.: Westview, 1981.

Chen, John H. M. *Vietnam: A Comprehensive Bibliography.* Metuchen, N.J.: Scarecrow, 1973.

Cincinnatus. *Self-Destruction: The Disintegration and Decay of the United States Army during the Vietnam Era.* New York: Norton, 1981.

Divine, Robert A. *Eisenhower and the Cold War.* New York: Oxford University, 1981.

Downs, Frederick. *The Killing Zone: My Life in the Vietnam War.* New York: Norton, 1978.

Emerson, Gloria. *Winners and Losers: Battles, Retreats, Gains, Losses, and Ruins from a Long War.* New York: Random House, 1976.

Figley, Charles R., and Seymour Leventman, eds. *Strangers at Home: Vietnam Veterans since the War.* New York: Praeger, 1980.

Gallucci, Robert L. *Neither Peace nor Honor: The Politics of American Military Policy in Vietnam.* Baltimore: Johns Hopkins University, 1975.

Gelb, Leslie H., and Richard K. Betts. *The Irony of Vietnam: The System Worked.* Washington, D.C.: Brookings Institution, 1979.

Goldstein, Joseph; Burke Marshall; and Jack Schwartz. *The My Lai Massacre and Its Coverup: Beyond the Reach of Law?* New York: Free Press, 1976.

Goodman, Allen E. *The Lost Peace: America's Search for a Negotiated Settlement of the Vietnam War.* Stanford, Calif.: Hoover Institution, 1978.

Griffen, William L., and John Marciano. *Teaching the Vietnam War: A Critical Examination of School Texts and an Interpretive Comparative History Utilizing the Pentagon Papers and Other Documents.* Totowa, N.J.: Littlefield, Adams, 1980.

Harrison, James Pinckney. *The Endless War: Fifty Years of Struggle in Vietnam.* New York: Free Press, 1982.

Helmer, John. *Bringing the War Home: The American Soldier in Vietnam and After.* New York: Free Press, 1974.

Herr, Michael. *Dispatches.* New York: Alfred A. Knopf, 1977.

Herring, George C. *America's Longest War: The United States and Vietnam, 1950–1975.* New York: Wiley, 1979.

Herring, George C., ed. *The Secret Diplomacy of the Vietnam War: The Negotiating Volumes of the Pentagon Papers.* Austin: The University of Texas Press, 1983.

Iriye, Akira, and Yonosuke Nagai. *The Origins of the Cold War in Asia.* New York: Columbia University Press, 1977.

Irving, R. E. M. *The First Indochina War: French and American Policy, 1945–1954.* London: Croom Helm, 1975.

Karnow, Stanley. *Vietnam: A History.* New York: Viking Press, 1983.

Kattenburg, Paul. *The Vietnam Trauma in American Foreign Policy, 1945–1975.* New Brunswick, N.J.: Transaction, 1980.

Kendrick, Alexander. *The Wound Within: America in the Vietnam Years, 1945–1974.* Boston: Little, Brown, 1974.

Kinnard, Douglas. *The War Managers*. Hanover, N.H.: University Press of New England, 1977.

Kovic, Ron. *Born on the Fourth of July*. New York: McGraw-Hill, 1976.

Lake, Anthony, ed. *The Legacy of Vietnam: The War, American Society, and the Future of American Foreign Policy*. New York: New York University Press, 1976.

Lewy, Guenter. *America in Vietnam*. New York: Oxford University Press, 1978.

Maclear, Michael. *The Ten Thousand Day War: Vietnam, 1945–1975*. New York: St. Martin's, 1981.

Millet, Allan, ed. *A Short History of the Vietnam War*. Bloomington: Indiana University Press, 1978.

Miroff, Bruce. *Pragmatic Illusions*. New York: McKay, 1976.

Patti, Aechimedes L. *Why Vietnam? Prelude to America's Albatross*. Berkeley: University of California Press, 1980.

Pisor, Robert. *The End of the Line: The Siege of Khe Sanh*. New York: Norton, 1982.

Podhoretz, Norman. *Why We Were in Vietnam*. New York: Simon and Schuster, 1982.

Porter, Gareth, ed. *Vietnam: A History in Documents*. New York: New American Library, 1979.

Porter, Gareth, ed. *A Peace Denied: The United States, Vietnam, and the Paris Agreements*. Bloomington: University of Indiana Press, 1975.

Ravenal, Earl C. *Never Again: Learning from America's Foreign Policy Failures*. Philadelphia: Temple University, 1978.

Rose, Lisle A. *Roots of Tragedy: The United States and the Struggle for Asia, 1945–1953*. Westport, Conn.: Greenwood, 1976.

Santoli, Al. *Everthing We Had: An Oral History of the Vietnam War by 33 American Soldiers Who Fought It*. New York: Random House, 1981.

Schandler, Herbert Y. *The Unmaking of a President: Lyndon Johnson and Vietnam*. Princeton: Princeton University Press, 1977.

Schell, Jonathan. *The Time of Illusion*. New York: Random House, 1974.

Shawcross, William. *Sideshow: Nixon, Kissinger, and the Destruction of Cambodia*. New York: Simon and Schuster, 1979.

Snepp, Frank. *Decent Interval: An Insider's Account of Saigon's Indecent End*. New York: Random House, 1977.

Tevens, Robert W. *Vain Hopes, Grim Realities: The Economic Consequences of the Vietnam War*. New York: New Viewpoints, 1967.

Szulc, Tad. *The Illusion of Peace: Foreign Policy in the Nixon Years*. New York: Viking, 1978.

Thies, Wallace J. *When Governments Collide: Coercion and Diplomacy in the Vietnam Conflict, 1964–1968*. Berkeley: University of California Press, 1980.

Thompson, James Clay. *Rolling Thunder: Understanding Policy and Pro-*

gram Failure. Chapel Hill: University of North Carolina Press, 1980.

Thomson, James C.; Peter W. Stanley; and John Curtis Perry. *Sentimental Imperialists: The American Experience in East Asia.* New York: Harper and Row, 1981.

Thompson, W. Scott, and Donaldson Frizzell, eds. *The Lessons of Vietnam.* New York: Crane-Russak, 1977.

Westmoreland, William C. *A Soldier Reports.* Garden City, N.Y.: Doubleday, 1976.

Wilmer, Harry A. *Dreams of Vietnam.* New York: Free Press, 1985.

Articles

Anderson, Robert S. "Operation Homecoming: Psychological Observations of Repatriated Vietnam Prisoners of War." *Psychiatry* 38, no. 1(1975): 65–74.

Arnold, Hugh M. "Official Justification for America's Role in Indochina, 1949–1967." *Asian Affairs: An American Review* 3, no. 1(1975): 31–48.

Bachman, Jerald D., and M. Kent Jennings. "The Impact of Vietnam on Trust in Government." *Journal of Social Issues* 31, no. 4(1975): 141–55.

Buchan, Alistair. "The Indochina War and World Politics." *Foreign Affairs* 53, no. 4(1975): 638–50.

Bundy, McGeorge. "Vietnam, Watergate, and Presidential Powers." *Foreign Affairs* 58, no. 2(1979–80): 397–407.

Burstein, Paul. "Senate Voting on the Vietnam War, 1964–1973: From Hawk to Dove." *Journal of Political and Military Sociology* 7, no. 2(1979): 271–82.

Ehrhart, William D. "Why I Did It." *Virginia Quarterly Review* 56, no. 1(1980): 19–31.

Fifield, Russell H. "The Thirty Years War in Indochina: A Conceptual Framework." *Asian Survey* 17, no. 9(1977): 857–79.

Herring, George C. "The Truman Administration and the Restoration of French Sovereignty in Indochina." *Diplomatic History* 1, no. 2(1977): 97–117.

Hess, Gary R. "The First American Commitment in Indochina: The Acceptance of the Bao Dai Solution." *Diplomatic History* 2, no. 3(1978): 331–50.

Hess, Gary R. "United States Policy and the Origins of the French-Vietminh War, 1945–1946." *Peace and Change* 3, no. 3(1975): 21–33.

Kahan, George M. "The Pentagon Papers: A Critical Evaluation." *American Political Science Review* 69, no. 3(1975): 675–84.

Katz, Mark N. "The Origins of the Vietnam War, 1945–1948." *Review of Politics* 42, no. 2(1980): 131–51.

LaFeber, Walter. "Roosevelt, Churchill, and Indochina, 1942–1945." *American Historical Review* 80, no. 5(1975): 1277–95.

Melby, John F. "Vietnam—1950." *Diplomatic History* 6, no. 1(1982): 97–109.

Mueller, John E. "The Search for the 'Breaking Point' in Vietnam: The Statistics of a Deadly Quarrel." *International Studies Quarterly* 24, no. 4(1980): 497–531.

Parker, Maynard. "Vietnam: The War That Won't End." *Foreign Affairs* 53, no. 1(1975): 352–74.

Pelz, Stephen. "Alibi Alley: Vietnam As History." *Reviews in American History* 8, no. 1(1980): 139–43.

Ravenal, Earl C. "Consequences of the End Game in Vietnam." *Foreign Affairs* 53, no. 4(1975): 651–57.

Reich, Dale. "One Year in Vietnam: A Young Soldier Remembers." *Wisconsin Magazine of History* 64, no. 3(1981): 162–80.

Roskin, Michael. "From Pearl Harbor to Vietnam: Shifting Generational Paradigms." *Political Science Quarterly* 89, no. 3(1974): 563–88.

Siracusa, Joseph M. "United States, Vietnam and the Cold War: A Reappraisal." *Journal of Southeast Asian Studies* 5, no. 1(1974): 91–108.

Taylor, Gordon O. "American Personal Narrative of the War in Vietnam." *American Literature* 52, no. 2(1980): 294–308.

Thompson, W. Scott. "The Indochinese Debacle and the United States." *Orbis* 19, no. 3(1975): 990–1011.

Contributors

Robert Bly's collections of poetry include *Silence on the Snowy Fields, The Light around the Body* (winner of the 1968 National Book Award), *The Morning Glory, This Tree Will Be Here for a Thousand Years, The Teeth Mother Naked at Last,* and *Sleepers Joining Hands,* among others. Bly was a cofounder in 1966 of American Writers against the Vietnam War and edited *A Poetry Reading against the Vietnam War.* His poetry journals, *The Fifties, The Sixties,* and *The Seventies,* published many European and South American poets for the first time in the United States. A graduate of Harvard, Bly resides in his native state of Minnesota.

Lynda E. Boose is assistant professor of English and teaches Shakespeare at the University of Texas at Austin. She received a B.A. degree from the University of New Mexico in 1969 and a Ph.D. degree from the University of California–Los Angeles in 1978. During the Vietnam-War era, Boose lived in Southeast Asia, where her husband had been assigned to the staff of the Naval Commander of Amphibious Operations operating out of Subic Bay Naval Base in the Philippines. From 1964 to 1966 she worked as head of the Household Goods Office at the Naval Supply Depot, where her responsibilities included shipping back the effects and remains of the deceased for United States Navy and Marine casualties and the belongings of MIA's in Vietnam.

Philip L. Geyelin is editor in residence of the Johns Hopkins Foreign Policy Institute. He was editor of the editorial page of the *Washington Post* from 1967 to 1978. He worked for the *Wall Street Journal* from 1947 to 1967, with early assignments covering the Dewey, Eisenhower, and Stevenson campaigns and the White

House. From 1956 to 1960 Geyelin was chief European correspondent for the *Wall Street Journal* in Paris and London, and he covered events in the Suez, Lebanon, Berlin, and Baghdad. From 1960 to 1966 he was the diplomatic correspondent in Washington for the *Wall Street Journal*, and he traveled to Vietnam, Cuba, the Dominican Republic, and Europe. He is the author of *Lyndon B. Johnson and the World* (1966) and numerous articles that have appeared in *Foreign Policy Magazine, Atlantic*, and other leading publications. Geyelin won a Pulitzer Prize for editorial writing in 1970.

George C. Herring is professor of history at the University of Kentucky, where he has taught since 1969. Herring holds a Ph.D. degree from the University of Virginia. He is the author of *Aid to Russia, 1941–1946: Strategy, Diplomacy, the Origins of the Cold War* (1973), and *America's Longest War: The United States and Vietnam* (1979). He is also editor of *The Diaries of Edward R. Stettinius, Jr., 1943–1946* (1975). His numerous articles have appeared in *Southern History, Journal of American History, Virginia Quarterly Review*, and *Southern Studies*.

Douglas Kinnard received a B.S. degree from the United States Military Academy. He held many command positions in ranks from junior officer through general officer until his voluntary retirement in 1970. His staff assignments included: assistant secretary of the Army General Staff (1957–59); speciai assistant to the Supreme Allied Commander Europe (1961–64); chief of operations analysis, U.S. Military Assistance Command, Vietnam (1966–67); office assistant for international security affairs to the secretary of defense (1967–68); and chief of staff of the Second Field Force in Vietnam (1969–70). He completed his Ph.D. degree in political science from Princeton University in 1973. From 1973 to 1983 he served as assistant professor, associate professor, and professor of political science at the University of Vermont. Author of *The Secretary of Defense* (1980), *The War Managers* (1977), and *President Eisenhower and Strategy Management* (1977), Kinnard is currently working on two manuscripts, *The Second Indochina War* and *Maxwell Taylor and the American Military Tradition*.

Walter W. Rostow is Rex G. Baker, Jr., Professor of Political Economy at the University of Texas at Austin. He holds B.A. and Ph.D. degrees from Yale University. He served as a major in the Office of Strategic Services during World War II. Early positions in government included assignments with the German-Austrian Economic Division of the State Department and with the Economic Commission for Europe. President Kennedy appointed Rostow as deputy special assistant for national security affairs in 1961 and, in 1962, as chairman of the Policy Planning Council of the Department of State. In 1966 Rostow returned to the White House as President Johnson's special assistant for national security affairs, a position held until January 20, 1969. He is the author of numerous books, including *A Design for Asian Development*; *View from the Seventh Floor*; *The Stages of Economic Growth, a Non-Communist Manifesto*; *The Process of Economic Growth*; *The American Diplomatic Revolution*; *The World Economy: History and Prospect*; *Getting from Here to There*; and a series of volumes entitled *Ideas and Action* exploring the making of major policy decisions. Rostow has held teaching positions at Oxford University, Cambridge University, and Massachusetts Institute of Technology.

James F. Veninga is executive director of the Texas Committee for the Humanities. He received his Ph.D. degree in history and religious studies from Rice University. He has held teaching positions at Middle Tennessee State University, University of St. Thomas (Houston), and the University of Texas at Austin. He has published many articles on the humanities and their role in public life. He is editor in chief of the *Texas Humanist* and edited a collection of essays, *The Biographer's Gift: Life Histories and Humanism*.

Harry A. Wilmer received M.D. and Ph.D. degrees from the University of Minnesota. He is founder, director, and president of the Institute for the Humanities at Salado and professor of psychiatry at the University of Texas Health Science Center in San Antonio. Before coming to Texas, Wilmer was professor of psychiatry at the Langley Porter Neuropsychiatric Institute, University of California, San Francisco. He previously taught at Stanford University and held a National Research Council Fellowship at Johns Hopkins

University. Awarded a Guggenheim Fellowship in 1969, Wilmer has written five books and over 150 medical articles. While on active duty in the United States Navy in the 1950s he worked with Korean War veterans. His book, *Social Psychiatry in Action*, dealt with his work at the naval hospital in Oakland and was made into an hour program on ABC television as the first show in the Alcoa Premier Series. His work with the nightmares and post-trauma stress of Vietnam veterans at the Audie Murphy Hospital in San Antonio is reported in his forthcoming book, *Dreams of Vietnam.*

Index